HEALING IN DEPTH

HEALING IN DEPTH

Culver M. Barker

Edited by H. I. Bach

HODDER AND STOUGHTON
LONDON SYDNEY AUCKLAND TORONTO

Preface

Dr. Culver Barker's *Healing in Depth* is one of the most impressive books on analytical psychology that has ever come my way. It is so singularly impressive because it conveys the living experience of the meaning of Jungian psychology in his own life as well as those of the hundreds who turned to him for help. Jung said once to me: 'Only the doctor who is affected himself by the plight of his patients can help. Only the wounded physician heals.'

Culver Barker had an unusual capacity for being wide open to the suffering of others and an unusual sense of what was wrong in our time and how the individual, however lonely and ostensibly unimportant, could serve to set it right. Jung was his point of departure but for him never became another 'ism'. Analytical psychology, he knew, was nothing if it did not enable the individual to find his own unique self as truly as Jung had found his own, and what makes Culver Barker's approach so valuable is that he did not find his own self without participating fully in the life of his time.

One certain sign of the healing integrity he brought to his work is the fact that he never writes outside his own experience. Implied in everything is the realisation that no doctor or teacher can take their human beings further than he has taken himself. As a result, he took himself so far that in my view there is no psychiatrist living who could afford to ignore this book or turn to it without being helped by it. What is more, there is no one who experiences the growing sickness of our time as a personal neurosis who will not benefit from reading this book.

I myself have always believed that the solution of the problems of our desperate day can only come from men and women who make the problems specific and accept them as their own challenge from life and a call to resolve it in their own seemingly drab round of existence. Culver Barker, and all the suffering people in this book who worked with him, prove for me that this belief was no idle fantasy, and it gives one more hope than ever for the future.

LAURENS VAN DER POST

Foreword

The collection of lectures and essays by the late Culver M. Barker may prove far more important than its slender volume and unassuming style might suggest.

Although in no way conceived as an introductory text, it provides uninitiated readers with an ideal approach to Analytical Psychology. The author takes them by the hand, as it were, presenting them first with a portrait of Jung, then with his own early experiences in a psychiatric ward, and finally with live situations in his consulting room. Here readers may find some of their own problems reflected and taken care of, with deep insight and a skill that is always tinged with sympathy.

The book's message to the specialist is no less important. Appearing ten years after the death of Jung, it provides a much needed orientation for the future of Analytical Psychology. Faced with a heritage of prodigious scope, those who set out by following Jung may quite naturally tend to concentrate on some aspects of his work while neglecting others. Thus there may be a stress on individual therapy which has little use for his great discovery of archetypal patterns; on the other hand, there may be a ceaseless search for collective features which pays perhaps insufficient attention to the personal situation and suffering in which they come to light — a tendency that might ultimately lead to an esoteric cult of the archetypal symbol. A similar trend towards either/or approaches may emerge in therapeutic method: some Post-Jungians may believe they have found the master key in the analysis of transference phenomena, while others remain almost exclusively devoted to the interpretation of dreams and active imagination. Certainly all these facets can be found in the Master's work. The situation is further complicated, however, by the unavoidably ambivalent attitude that arises upon the passing of a great man, for a dedicated adherence to the founder's views may come into conflict with a felt need for development and progress.

On all these issues the wisdom of the present author provides sure guidance. While holding on to the essentials of Jung's teaching, he has broken new ground with his concepts of 'original hurt' and 'healing in depth'. As his case material illustrates, he takes note of all manifestations of the unconscious, whether it reveals itself through dreams, active imagination or in the transference. And while his own specific contribution focuses on critical events in a person's biography, he never fails to pay heed to the relevance of their archetypal dimension.

Viewed against the background of post-Jungian dilemmas, Culver Barker's writings exemplify a blending of elements that may well be on the way to becoming divisive issues. His work thus testifies to the fruitfulness of an 'integrated' approach. How did he achieve it? Partly, no doubt, because he never pursued theory for theory's sake but was motivated throughout by a supreme concern for the well-being of his patients. Thus he could adopt from physical science the concept of 'feed-back' and apply it in his psychotherapeutical sessions as long as it helped a sick soul towards recovery. Ultimately, however, the secret is to be found in his own personality which had attained to a rare measure of integration, making it possible for him to dispense with identifications and to accept whatever the phenomena would reveal to him. It is these truly Jungian qualities which give the pages that follow their distinctive character.

PAUL SELIGMAN

Dr. Paul Seligman, Professor of Philosophy, University of Waterloo, is the President of the Analytical Psychology Society of Ontario, Canada.

Contents

Introduction

Culver Maynard Barker was born in Sandown, Isle of Wight, on 4th March, 1891. He lost his mother at an early age and was brought up by two aunts; the holidays at his grandfather's estate were the highlights of his young life. When he reached adolescence, his father took him for high school education to Vancouver, British Columbia, where the family had settled. As a young man he joined a group who surveyed the uncharted lands of Northern British Columbia and the Yukon for the building of railways. The experience of the virgin land, with its deep-frozen ground beneath, its wide horizon and the high sky above, left a lasting impression on him. Up to his last years he would draw strength from staying at his cottage in a lonely spot high up on the Devon moors: the landscape, so dear to him, and the simple, frugal life there reminded him of his formative years. Having studied engineering he returned to England during the First World War with the engineers of the Second Canadian Division and, commissioned, saw active service in France.

At the end of the war he sensed the opportunity to reorientate his life. From his own experience as a half-orphaned boy, the most urgent task, socially, that he could envisage for himself was to contribute to the healthy development of children and to investigate the factors supporting it or interfering with it. He chose medicine, rather than law or education, as being fundamentally the most helpful to his end.

He studied at Pembroke College, Cambridge, and at University College Hospital, London. After various house appointments, for instance one at Manor House Hospital, where he introduced splints for dressing fractures, Dr. Barker decided on the Whitechapel Observation Ward of St. Peter's Hospital as being the most likely place to observe the broader spectrum of disturbances of the personality: it was the first in England to have a visiting psychiatrist, Dr. E. Mapother, Superintendent of the Maudsley Hospital. In those days, patients admitted to an observation ward were sorted out, either to be certified and then sent on to a mental institution wherever a bed was available, or else to be discharged to where they came from: no treatment or after-care were provided for. Between 1929 and 1935 Dr. Barker created at this then poor law Hospital the first psychotherapeutic out-patients' unit outside the teaching hospitals.

He had first met C. G. Jung in 1927, and he was seconded for an academic year to work with him in Zurich where he met his American-born wife, Mary. He later went over again repeatedly and kept in contact with Jung till the latter's death in 1961. The psychotherapeutic out-patient 'clinic', however, was the first fruit of Dr. Barker's newly-won psychological insight. 'No facilities were available for this work,' he recalled, 'it was unofficial and quite unsanctioned. To be engaged in activities outside the hospital routine, such as talking tête-à-tête, and again some days later, to a lady ex-patient, seated with our backs in the corridor joining the main hall to the midwifery ward, the quietest, the most private place available, was considered somewhat strange and even suspicious.' It was in this pioneering work in the East End of London that Dr. Barker first experienced the healing power of psychotherapy, the clinical value of a sequence of dreams and the potency of spontaneous paintings. The importance of his work was recognised by his report on it being included in the L.C.C. Report of 1937.

He left his post at the observation ward to go to the Cassel Hospital and then took up private practice. Perceiving early on that child, parents and environment are intimately interlinked, he worked at the same time at the London Child Guidance Clinic, then still in its beginnings, and later at the Institute of Child Psychology, where he was psychotherapist to both the Children's and Parents' Department. Other appointments included a clinical assistantship at the Department of Medical Psychology of University College Hospital.

During the last war, when having to give convulsion treatment at a mental hospital, then by chemical means—a horrifying experience for both patient and doctor—Dr. Barker saw an E.C.T. research machine at the Burden Institute, Bristol, and immediately ordered for himself the first that came on the market. Having *carte blanche* in its use for the patients in this large hospital, he once more had the opportunity of introducing a new method of treatment to otherwise untreated patients. This experimental physical approach, in particular when combined with psychotherapy, gave sometimes unexpectedly satisfying results. Once,

when called to a private patient during an air raid, he found him
in the air-raid shelter, and with the help of an electric extension,
the E.C.T. was given there.

In the field of psychiatry and psychotherapy, one of his main
contributions, based on the insight won from his own early experience, was his conception of 'healing in depth' and his approach
to 'critical' traumas in the growing years. These, he showed, frequently determine the later choice of vocation and tempt one to
give to others what one would urgently need oneself. He evolved a
special method of treatment which he called 'feed-back'. Even
though his concept of 'critical hurt' may superficially resemble the
trauma theory of neurosis and psychosis, his treatment of it
differs decisively from mere historical anamnesis or interpretation.
By tracing the continuing effects of such early injuries up to the
present and attending to these younger parts of the personality,
often emerging personified, he re-established contact between the
adult of today and those shut-off portions and could thus bring
healing to the crippling damage. He presented his ideas and the
results of treatment at the First International Congress for Analytical Psychology (Zurich, 1958).

During the last decade of his life, Dr. Barker took an active part
in a research project at the University Neurosurgical Clinic,
Zurich, on the evaluation of spontaneous paintings of severely ill
patients which gave striking evidence of the interrelation between
body and mind, and between the conscious and the unconscious
world. As this relationship was his deepest concern, the understanding of dreams as guides and helpers — as he once said, 'a manifesta-
tion of the caring one tending his hand' — remained the centre of his
attention. The responsible work he devoted to his patients' dreams
he also gave to his own.

He was a well-beloved lecturer at the C. G. Jung Institute,
Zurich and one of its Patrons, President of the Analytical
Psychology Club, Founder Member of, and Honorary Physician
to, the Society of Analytical Psychology, and Honorary Member
of the Guild of Pastoral Psychology, all in London.

Culver Barker died on 11th September, 1967. He was an
unassuming man of rare integrity and wisdom, at ease with people
from many walks of life. Keenly interested, he liked to hear of
their work and experiences, and even the shy and withdrawn
responded readily and frankly. His intuitive grasp of people and
situations was complemented by an engineer's and physician's
practical, down-to-earth approach. Always open to new explorations and methods that would deepen our comprehension of man

and his soul, he also kept track of a surprising range of scientific and technical fields far beyond his own, and he retained the freshness of his questioning mind to the last. He was for ever fascinated by the motive forces of human action, the way things are made and how they work.

Patients and colleagues in many lands felt him to be a real friend, a healing presence and, ever so often, a father such as they had never had before. With his gift of quick understanding and deep sympathy, he would 'talk to the situation', rarely in danger of losing sight of the human being over theories or preconceived ideas, firmly insisting that analysis should serve life but not become a substitute for it. His long clinical experience prevented him from overlooking physical symptoms in seemingly psychic disorders but likewise the psychological side in apparently specific somatic complaints. Capable of accepting his own limitations and possible mistakes, he was true to himself to an exceptional degree. He kept his youthful zest, his delightful sense of humour and, as C. G. Jung reciprocated in a personal letter, what Dr. Barker had seen as his chief characteristic: his humanness.

This volume endeavours to give a living reflection of his personality and the development of his insights and work, so far as possible in chronological order. Most of his papers were lectures, and only some have been printed before: 'Psychotherapy in the Observation Ward' in *The Lancet* (Vol. 233, No. 5945 of 7.8.1937); 'Some Positive Values of Neurosis' as Lecture No. 50 of the Guild of Pastoral Psychology, London (February 1947). A very condensed version of 'Healing in Depth' read to the First International Congress for Analytical Psychology, was published in its Proceedings (*Current Trends in Analytical Psychology* ed. G. Adler, London, 1961). 'Relating to the Centre' was a contribution to *Contact with Jung* (ed. M. Fordham, London, 1963). The editors' permission to reprint these papers is gratefully acknowledged.

I also wish to thank Dr. Barker's patients and students from whose analytical work he drew many examples. He used code names in all his notes, and their identity could not be ascertained. Those whose consent he might not have expressly obtained may be gratified to see what, beyond their own experience and benefit, their common work gave to him to hand on. Above all, I would like to express my gratitude to Susan R. Bach for her analytical grasp, steady co-operation and constructive help.

H.I.B.

I

C. G. Jung, the Man
and his work

I

As far as I can, I would like to give a picture of Professor Jung as the *man*, C. G. Jung. His works are there for us and future generations to read. Those who have worked with and know him may, however, be able to convey some personal aspects of this man, which from his writings alone can hardly be gathered, in his essential humanness, the glow and fibre of his personality, as well as of the background in which his work germinated and came into fruition. Having had the privilege to study analytical psychology under him in Zurich and having been in contact with him for over thirty years, I shall endeavour to convey something of the living personality, the human being, and some of his work as it arose out of his personal struggles and of his experience and research as a physician, a scientist and a scholar. Every time I look into the detail of his life and work and try to grasp it as a whole, I am amazed at both the immensity of the man as a man, and the extent of his achievement in his work.

Jung was a big man in every way, physically big and massive yet of a certain athletic leanness. In personality and mind he extended in height upwards and in depth downwards.

In spite of the size of his life's canvas and the scholarly scientific artistry with which he has painted his life on it, it was essentially made up of the ordinary tensions and counter-tensions such as yours or mine, but with that unique enrichment which I would like to call the spirit of Jung.

The Swiss background

C. G. Jung was born near Basle in 1875, the son of a long line of Protestant pastors and theologians and several physicians. I have often thought that only in Switzerland could have been produced such a balanced and comprehensive psychological system as Jung's where opposites blend into a new and more inclusive synthesis. This island of relative security and armed neutrality, in the centre of Europe is neither French, German nor Italian, yet the potential values of these countries are here available, each culture making its individual contribution.

Is it too much to see an interrelationship between C. G. Jung's personality and greatness and this special geographical and cultural situation, out of which he grew and in which he found support enabling him to produce his deep, rich, comprehensive and far-reaching psychology of the human mind? I might refer here to the recurrent vision* he had in 1913 of Switzerland being an island, surrounded by blood and with fire lapping its shores. The significance of the terrifying experience of this dream was only understood in its outer reality when war broke out in 1914. In a tribal setting a dream of this extent, quality and precision would be characteristic of the chief or medicine man.

Early dreams†

From a very early age, Jung felt that he was under a power greater than himself. This can be readily grasped by the fact that already at the age of four he had dreams of a profound and basic nature which he vividly remembered and held throughout his life. In a dream at this early age he saw a square hole in the field alongside his childhood home from which steps led down into an underground chamber. There he saw a red carpet leading to a throne or altar on which was placed a shape which, in later years, he realised represented the symbol of creativity. Still within the dream he heard his mother's voice commenting negatively on the central figure. Thus, perhaps, waking up, he did not mention the dream; in fact, he told no one about it until many decades later.

At the age of twelve he had another stupendous dream which shook him so deeply that for three days and nights he wrestled with the temptation to forget it. But this boy felt tested by God and finally won through to an acceptance that God wanted him to see and stand up for things in a way different from that of his fathers and forefathers, however terrifying and challenging that might be. After accepting the dream as his dream in this way, the doubts and fears faded and a deep sense of assuredness, undoubtedness, was with him; he knew now he was a person in his own right and was called upon to obey his inner voice.

To me this was without doubt a spontaneous initiation

*C. G. Jung, *Memories, Dreams, Reflections*. Recorded and edited by Aniela Jaffé (Collins and Routledge, London 1963), p. 169.
†Ibid., pp. 25 et seq., 49 et seq.

experience such as we find in religious history and which initiation rites attempt to bring about. Maybe this can help us to comprehend how he was able, again and again, to stand by himself for the truth as it called to him.

Clash with parents

One of the early occasions on which a very characteristic quality of his spirit appeared, namely a courageous search for truth regardless of convention or authority, was a clash at the age of ten with his father, whose portrait in Dr. Jung's private library gave me the impression of a man of intensity and Swiss integrity. He asked his father, who was a clergyman, why, if God is almighty, he allows the Devil to wander about tripping people up, when any of the neighbours who had a dog that interfered like that would be punished and the dog chained up or destroyed. His father was unable to answer this awkward question adequately for the searching mind of this intelligent boy. In his esteem, his father did shrink when, not unnaturally, he could not stand up to his searching question. Jung has said that ever since, when talking to a man much older than himself, he had to add at least ten per cent to his estimate of him because he might be tempted to depreciate him, so deep and lasting was the shock.

The difficulties which the boy had to face, to relate to and to live with, were much the same as those of other people and not of his own making, but he took them on as a challenge. The first and not least of these was his own parents, both vivid and dynamic but very different personalities, so that, from his childhood onwards, he was forged between what later he called the tension of opposites. His father, a kindly man, happy with the daily round among his parishioners, according to his son apparently never developed the gifts and abilities which may have attracted Jung's mother when they first met. She, on the other hand, had had an unusually wide education for those days and may have found the simple life of her husband frustrating and most likely not up to her expectations. The boy found her fascinating but completely unpredictable. In so far as the adolescent, in a critical respect, could not have the needful confidence in his father's relationship to God or in his mother's acceptance of himself, he was what I would call orphaned; and so, to obtain a rightful security and necessary belongingness to life, he needed most profoundly to find a direct relationship to his centre, to the mystery of life and being, which is not ordinarily demanded of one to whom this is mediated by the parents.

Student years

Jung, as a student at Basle, took up archaeology and philosophy, but soon changed to medicine, although keeping up his philosophical studies and interests. He has said that all the chief decisions of his life have been supported by dreams, which includes his change-over to medicine.

It was at the age of twenty-one, when he and a group of friends experimented with seances, becoming interested in the phenomena of a mediumistic girl, that Jung decided to investigate what went on behind the mind. Working for his final medical examination, he picked up a standard textbook on psychiatry and, he said, the first page made his heart beat with excitement, and by the second page he was completely caught up with the idea that in this realm he could find the answers to the questions which the girl medium had posed for him. He there and then decided within himself to become a psychiatrist. Actually it was the last thing he had intended to take up, not least so, he said, because his father was interested in it, being a pastor to the Canton Mental Hospital in Zurich, and, as Jung then felt, 'sons think that what their fathers are interested in can't be up to much.'

He passed first in his examinations. He had been earmarked by teachers and friends for a brilliant career in orthodox clinical medicine. A university post in general medicine awaited him, and his friends and colleagues were amazed when he decided to take up what was then considered a very outlandish and unprogressive speciality, i.e. psychiatry.

He was in his early twenties and was working on his word-association tests when he came to a critical clash with his mother. The walls of his study were covered with the grotesque lines of differently coloured graphs. Jung was totally immersed in this, his first adult research. The tender growing point of scientific creation was exposed and vulnerable when his mother came into the room and exclaimed: 'Do you think that this means something?' This so shook him, sent him into confusion and doubt, that for three weeks he was demoralised and unable to work on. Then he rallied and went back to his work—and, I am sure, more purposefully than before.

Word-association tests

Jung's development of word-association tests led to rather striking results. He demonstrated that, in reply to a stimulus word, the reaction time, if prolonged, indicated emotional interference, activated by what he found to be an unconscious reaction.

Such unconscious interferences were 'autonomous' in the sense of not being subject to conscious control, and this led him to the description of what he called a psychological 'complex'—a term that has been taken over into everyday use in many European languages.

Jung became very adept with this method of discovering repressed contents; on several occasions he was called in by the Zurich police to interview suspected criminals, with successful results, and in a less serious context, when applying it to colleagues who lent themselves to the experiments, he discovered to their surprise and I daresay embarrassment that one of them had a love affair in a neighbouring town which he had cunningly concealed. The method is still taught at the University College of Zurich, the Eidgenössische Technische Hochschule, as an introduction to the significance and power of emotion in the individual, though Jung himself later abandoned it in analytical therapy, as he found he could get the same material, but in a more comprehensive form, from the analysis of patients' dreams. At any rate, he had found one clue to what he had been looking for, namely what went on behind the mind, and to the question he had asked himself much earlier: 'Who are the intruders of the mind?'

Jung and Freud

This work on the word-association tests established the scientific reputation of Jung who was then working with a team as Senior Psychiatrist at the County Mental Hospital, the 'Burghölzli'. At the same time, Freud in Vienna had reached his first important conclusions on psychoanalysis, namely the discovery of a realm called the unconscious and the significance of its effect of repression. In contradistinction to Jung's then increasing academic standing, Freud's theories met with hostile reception or even with complete disregard. However, Jung was impressed by finding someone else who acknowledged the importance of the psyche in itself and was also interested in the hidden forces behind it as well as by Freud's theoretical comprehension. At that time he accepted the theory of repression of forbidden contents and told Freud of his own experimental results which supported this theory. In Jung's own words:

'I was planning an academic career and was about to complete a work that would advance me in the University. Freud, definitely *persona non grata* in the medical world of that time, was hardly mentioned above a whisper by people of importance. At the Congresses he was discussed only in the corridors, never on the floor, and any connection with him was a menace to one's own reputation.

'Therefore, the discovery by me that my experiments in association were directly confirming Freud's theories of repression was most unwelcome. One time, while working in my laboratory, it flashed into my mind that Freud had actually elaborated a theory which would explain my experiments. At the same time, a devil whispered in my ear that I could perfectly well publish my work without mentioning Freud, that I had worked out my experiments long before I knew of him, and so could claim complete independence of him as far as they went. However, I saw at once that it would be an evasion which I did not propose to go in for.'*

It was in 1907 that he actually met Freud, and he gives a moving account of this first meeting.† Jung states that Freud was the first man of real stature that he had met: 'No one else could compare with him.' They met one day at one p.m. and talked steadily for thirteen hours. In later months they travelled and lectured together and analysed each other's dreams.

'I openly took up the cudgels for Freud,' as Jung puts it. 'In 1904 there was a Congress at Munich on the subject of compulsion neuroses, and mention of Freud's work was omitted. This time I wrote an article in a well-known German medical journal defending Freud. Immediately a flood of resistances was released against me, and two professors wrote me letters warning me that my academic future was at stake if I persisted in joining forces with Freud. Of course, I felt that if I had to get an academic future at such a price, it could be damned, and I went on writing about Freud.'

From his first interview with Freud, although he was overwhelmingly impressed by him, Jung had come away with a certain amount of doubt, first about the complete omnipotence of Freud's sexual theory, and secondly about Freud himself. There seemed a strange emotion when Freud talked about sex, almost as if he were talking about God. The deep bitterness with which Freud often spoke also made Jung wonder about his inner freedom.

But the first serious disagreement came when Jung was analysing a dream of Freud's on a journey to America to lecture. Freud said he could not give certain associations which would have helped in the interpretation, because to do so would undermine his authority. After that Jung never analysed another dream of Freud's. Again, when Jung brought in examples of neurosis in which the sexual

*This passage, and the following, are quoted from Jung's Seminar of 1925 (to be published by Princeton University Press).

†*Memories, Dreams, Reflections*, p. 146 et seq.

aspect, if any, seemed to be entirely secondary, Freud would call it, say, psycho-sexuality and then, by drawing out thread after thread, finally reduce it to nothing but sexuality. What Jung deprecated and felt most destructive is to reduce something to 'nothing but'.

Apart from such divergencies, Jung also experienced unconscious reactions. He said: 'As Freud could only partially handle my dreams, the amount of symbolic material in them increased, as it always does until it is understood. If one remains with a too narrow point of view about the dream material, there comes a feeling of dissociation and one feels blind and deaf. When this happens to an isolated man, he petrifies.'

Jung was considered and talked of as the obvious heir and successor of Freud. At that time Freud thought and believed that the unconscious was an undifferentiated stream, as it were: 'The unconscious can only wish.' Jung's demonstration, in the *Psychology of the Unconscious*, of its duality, of its yea and nay (now known as 'the opposites'), that is, of its compensatory nature, was anathema to Freud's monistic conception of it. The publication of this book in 1912 led to a complete break with Freud which was never healed.

The separation was, therefore, not on petty grounds but on basic principles which involved Jung's integrity for truth as he saw and felt it, his being true to the psyche as it manifested itself and to the dream facts, no matter how uncomfortable to the pride and comfort of the ego they might be.

This break with Freud involved severe repercussions to Jung's standing as a teacher, scholar and psychiatrist. Many of his students, by then drawn from all parts of the world to study the new Freudian psychology, left him. To his colleagues he became nothing but a mystic, and this attitude to his pioneering work continued almost up to the present time. I remember well how, shortly before the First World War, it was said at a meeting of the British Psychological Society: 'What a pity Jung has given up psychiatry and gone into mysticism.' At another psychological meeting of the London Child Guidance Clinic, two psychiatrist friends of mine whom I had known at the university came up to me and said: 'Oh, here is that queer duck who knows Jung.'

Jung's book on Types and the four functions

Jung at this stage found himself in conflict both with Freud and Alfred Adler. It is characteristic of his scientific spirit that he set to work to investigate the puzzling fact that up to a point the same dream material could with apparent consistency and fitness be interpreted in two quite different ways. Jung demonstrated that there was a third interpretation which, while not excluding the others, extended the appreciation of the dream situation both in width and depth. Instead of becoming bitter and resentful at the contradiction of both these schools to his own conception, he used this seeming incompatibility as an occasion for querying and clarifying the foundations of his own as well as his opponents' views. The effort to understand their different approach, and to do justice to all three of them, led to his book on *Types*. This attitude of taking on a conflict situation of his own as a challenge, of including himself and what conditioned him, is typical of Jung's courageous humbleness. It was in this endeavour to grasp the differences between Freud, Adler and himself that he coined the terms extravert and introvert which now have become household words, the one being orientated more towards the object outside, the other being conditioned by his own inner reaction to the outer world. It should be emphasised here that in Jung's conception and in one's own experience these two attitudes are complementary — they are not mutually exclusive, and both are necessary for a satisfactory relationship to any situation or person.

The insight by which Jung came to understand such differences was founded on his recognition of *four basic functions*, thinking, feeling, intuition and sensation, which we all have and use in varying degrees to relate to reality. It is the relative predominance, or lesser development, of each of these functions that determines the great variety of existing types. I may quote Jung himself on the intuitive function: 'You see, you get your orientation, you get your bearings in the chaotic abundance of impressions by the four functions, four aspects; so, if you can tell me any other aspect by which you get your orientation, I'm very grateful. I haven't found more. I tried. But those are the four that covered the thing. For instance, the intuitive type, which is very little understood, has a very important function because he is the one going by hunches, he sees around corners, he smells a rat a mile away. He can give you perception and orientation in a situation where your senses, your intellect and your feeling are no good at all. When you are in an absolute fix, an intuition can show you the hole through which you can escape. This is a very important function under primitive conditions or wherever you are confronted with vital issues you cannot master by rules or by logic.'

Dreams in Jung's and Freud's view

In speaking of the difference of approach between Jung and

Freud, it may be illuminating to compare it in relation to dreams. Both stress the importance of dreams in the effort to reach a relationship with the unconscious, but in their attitude, valuation and interpretation they differ profoundly. To Freud, conditioned as he was by the materialistic psychology of the 1880s with its insistence on the pleasure principle as the main drive, dreams were above all the fulfilment of wishes which could not be gratified owing to repression by conscious censorship, namely the taboo imposed by civilisation on what is now known as the Oedipus complex. This is to say, he understood and interpreted dreams chiefly by ultimate reference to the urge of the son to overcome the father so as to possess the mother. Jung, on the other hand, observed and demonstrated that contents and meaning of dreams are far more comprehensive than this. Both Freud and Jung noticed that the contents of dreams come from layers differing in depth; on the one hand, those that refer more to the dreamer's personal circumstances and conditions, on the other hand, figures and motifs appear which have no such direct and readily seen connections with the dreamer. Freud called this second, deeper layer of the unconscious its 'archaic' stratum and did not consider it to be of any importance for the understanding of dreams, in line with his recognising only a personal unconscious, although he, too, used parallels from the history of religions and from anthropological research.

The collective unconscious

Jung discovered in this deeper layer of the unconscious a realm which is common to all mankind regardless of race, colour or social pattern. He called it the collective unconscious, as distinct from the personal, being shared by humans throughout all the ages and civilisations. Although we recognise since Darwin that we have common ancestors even far beyond Abraham, it was a staggering discovery of Jung's to find the parallel to the biological continuity in the spiritual and psychological field. His insight came out of his daily practical work with patients. Yet beyond studying and collecting the dreams of his patients, who came by then once again from all parts of the world, and finding corresponding motifs in them, he checked on his findings extensively, travelled to New York hospitals to study the dreams of Negroes, to the Pueblo Indians of New Mexico, to central and eastern Africa and to India. Moreover, he found in the history of religions, in mythology and anthropology parallels which gave him clues to the understanding of his patients' dreams and phantasies that otherwise would have remained incomprehensible to them as well as to him.

Archetypes

This endeavour and the need to investigate so many apparently remote fields misled some people into calling him a mystic where, as a true scientific worker, he was searching for parallels in comparable disciplines. In fact, grasping myths and fairy tales as the dreams of mankind, he reached through them the same common stratum as in the imagery of his individual patients and could thus understand it better by using age-old legends or fairy tales to amplify his clinical observations. Their recurrence in certain critical situations for which they are typical, prompted Jung to call them *archetypes*, a term which he found in Greek literature already as denoting the eternal images.

For example, Jung recalls* the experience with one particular patient who, in the course of her treatment, projected on to him the all-powerful father figure. Though intellectually she knew this to be absurd, yet an inner need kept her under this spell. When Jung was in this dilemma and pondering how to resolve it, she brought a significant dream: Jung stood in a field of wheat, an enormous field of wheat that was ripe for harvest. He was a giant, and he held her in his arms like a baby, and the wind was blowing over that field of wheat. She felt as being in the arms of a god. This was for him the moment to interpret: 'Now the harvest is ripe, and I must tell her.' So he told her: 'You see, what you want and what you project into me because you are not conscious of it in yourself is the idea of a deity—you see it in me.' The idea of a deity is not an intellectual idea. It is a fundamental human experience, inborn— an archetype. Jung was the wheat himself. He was the spirit of the wheat—the spirit of the wind, and she was in the arms of that divine presence. And in her dream she had the living experience of an archetype. It made a tremendous impression upon that girl. She saw what she was really missing. 'The power that she had seen in me', Jung said, 'was within herself—within reach through the dream. As long as that missing value was projected into me, it made me indispensable to her. The dream was a fundamental religious, a numinous experience' which now she was able to grasp, to accept and even to hold. You see, if one reaches this layer at a moment of openness of heart and mind, be it through a religious experience, at a creative moment of an artist or in a

*C. G. Jung, 'Two Essays on Analytical Psychology', *Collected Works* (Routledge, London, 1953/1966), Vol. 7, para. 211.

personal analysis, one has touched the common ground of life and humanity and can begin to live from there, and with it a sense of basic belongingness can begin to develop.

One must not think that the work of a psychotherapist, even of Jung, always reaches such depth. I remember a story he told. A young man, a university student, came to him for help who had become unable to work for his final. When asked what worried him he said he was engaged to be married to a girl of whom he thought very highly and was quite happy, but in dreams he was greatly disturbed—he saw his fiancée going out with other men while he was swatting. As a good analyst, Jung carefully investigated the dreams and the total situation, and finally said: 'Well, perhaps your dreams are right in outer reality—what about finding out?' To cut a long story short, the young man sought the help of a private detective who, without any particular difficulty, found out that she was indeed going with other men—in fact, she was a prostitute. The relief from the uncertainty set him free to work, and he passed his exam. This advice and its result brings out vividly an important ingredient of Jung's character, his down-to-earth Swiss common sense.

Jung faces his own irrational side

On the other hand, Jung had the integrity to ask for his own part in his researches as well as in his daily work. After writing his book, *The Psychology of the Unconscious*, based on Miss Miller's phantasies, with its wealth of unconscious material, which led him to his profound researches on mythological motifs and their significant relationship to the human psyche, Jung had asked himself: 'What does this mean to *me*?', and in this way he came to examine his own unconscious. In an early Seminar he states what it meant to a thinker to face the irrational: 'To a man in whom thinking is the developed function, facing his irrational side is highly repellent'—that is how it initially felt to him to accept the irrational as part of himself. To illustrate what it meant to him to meet the irrationality of his own inferior side, then still in the shadow, I will quote the passage in full:

'I was in my conscious an active thinker, accustomed to subject my thoughts to the most rigorous sort of direction. Therefore, phantasy as a mental process was directly repellent to me. As a form of thinking, I held it to be altogether impure, a sort of incestuous intercourse, thoroughly immoral from an intellectual viewpoint. Admitting phantasy in myself had the same effect on me as would be produced on a man if he came into his workshop and found all his tools flying about independent of his will. In other words, it shocked me to think of the possibility of a phantasy life in my own mind; it was against all the intellectual ideals I had developed in myself, and so great was my resistance that I could only admit the fact to myself through the process of projecting my material into Miss Miller's. Or, to put it even more strongly, passive thinking seemed to me such a weak and perverted thing that I could only handle it through a diseased woman.

'I had to pick up the other side, the passive side of my mental life. A man dislikes to do this because he feels himself so helpless. He can't quite manage it and he feels inferior. It is as though he were a log being tossed about in a stream, and so he gets out of it as soon as possible. He repudiates it because it is not pure intellect; even worse than that, it might be feeling. He feels himself a victim of all that, and yet he must deliver himself over to it in order to get at his creative power. Since my anima had been definitely awakened by all the mythological material I had been working with, I was forced now to give attention to that other side, to my unconscious, the inferior side in other words. This sounds very easy, I know, but it is a statement a man hates to make. This other side of his thinking is not repellent to a woman, particularly to a certain sort of woman. I think of women as belonging in general to types, the mother and the hetaira. The hetaira type acts as the mother for the other side of man's thinking. The very fact of its being a weak and helpless sort of thinking appeals to this sort of woman, she thinks of it as something embryonic which she helps to develop.'

This gives you some idea of what it meant to a man of Jung's quality and temperament to be a pioneer in this world of the irrational, the unconscious. In this we can get a vivid realisation of what we mean by Jung's spirit and the relationship between the man and his work. After having achieved the writing of a highly original and very complex work, a lesser man might well have allowed himself to sit back and rest on this attainment. But no — without any external prompting, C. G. Jung went straight on and asked himself what this had to do with him. It needed his outstanding courage and humility to stand by his sense of total truth. We should try to recognise the cost and suffering which it meant to him and the continuity of 'work' on himself that it has involved throughout his life. To us who through him are now acquainted with the irrational and feel it is a proud achievement to relate to it, it is only to a very small degree possible to realise what he himself went through.

This courageous attitude was not confined to Jung's researches but he also lived it in his daily analytical work, as the following happening* strikingly illustrates. He was consulted by a woman who was duly shown into his consulting room in his private house in Zurich-Küsnacht. As she entered, he could hardly believe his eyes because her appearance was quite staggering in this setting: she was dressed up, painted and scented as would only be found among the *demi-mondes* of that time. Jung said: 'I was really ashamed of her coming to my house and the maid having to show her in.' That night he had a dream in which this woman stood raised above him, superior to him in attitude and raiment while he, from down below, was looking up to her. This dream indicated sharply to him that whatever her outer appearance and his collective prejudices, he had grossly underestimated her essential personality. Jung said that, at the next consultation — and I am sure after some deep consideration — he decided to tell her his dream with, as he added, quite satisfactory results as to establishing a sound therapeutic relationship.

By taking on his own problems and difficulties, Jung has become a guide and his insight a healing factor in our daily life. We owe it to him that we can today ask: what is the significance, the meaning of, say, a dream or a phantasy, what does it tend to convey to us for the sake of a healthy and fuller life? In attempting to live somewhat in Jung's spirit, we have to be ready to take on in our own way some comparable struggle and do so truthfully in accordance with our individual potentials.

The shadow

What Jung called the shadow aspect of the personality goes far beyond Freud's conception of the unconscious as the container of repressed contents and forbidden wishes, for it includes also dormant and undeveloped possibilities such as latent gifts and positive character traits. He recognised this shadow aspect not only in others, which is relatively easy, but in himself. To his eternal distinction and with courage beyond belief he brought it into his consciousness, and as far as he could into his range of living. The recognition of the shadow aspect of the human personality with all its undiscovered values in the still dark of the unconscious has been one of his greatest contributions: 'Only a ghost casts no shadow.' If one can be helped and dare to recognise these as qualities of one's own potential self and total nature, then they could strengthen the undernourished component of our everyday existence. If people

*Cf. C. G. Jung, 'Two Essays on Analytical Psychology'. *Collected Works*, Vol. 7, para. 189.

can be assisted, for instance by analysis, to revalue themselves, their shadow ceases to be a permanent threat that has to be held down by will-power and may, as it were, become a friend from whom to draw support and strength. There are jewels to be found in this often repellent and forbidding darkness.

We might well ask: how could a man, single-handed as it were, unsupported by a fellow-analyst, withstand the forces of the unconscious that were aroused in his depth in this pioneering work? The answer may partly be found in that Jung, in these years, had built up an ego of great stability and integrity. The ego is the servant of the psyche. By relating to and co-operating with these powers from within with sincerity and regardless of prestige, he enlisted their support and co-operation. He had faced the challenges of the outer world as they came up, and met them in relationship to his innermost centre. For the sake of this truth he had on more than one occasion left the warmth and security of relationship with his colleagues to go into the wilderness, and so his ego had become tempered by meeting adversity and had thus reached a high degree of maturity. This in the subsequent years, I believe, enabled him to meet the impact of the activation of the unconscious which had been brought about by his outstanding conscious development in relation to it. An example which we all need in this field is the wise care that he took in regard to his own necessities, giving with both hands as a physician and teacher but, at other times, assigning full priority to his own personal needs.

In facing the irrational and shadow side of himself, Jung became critically aware of the wide gulf between intellectual understanding and the *living comprehension* which comes from experience in which heart, mind and body have partaken. I would like to say here that those who seek help and enrichment in Jung's insight and writings need to remind themselves of what he mentions only briefly and what therefore can only too easily be evaded or forgotten: namely, that he writes primarily for those who live, suffer and experience the various responsibilities of life on the way to reaching a mature personality. It is easy to be tempted to reach out intellectually for the fruit of such maturity while neglecting the arduous and painful task of working out, step by step, in everyday life, the immature aspects of ourselves, those disturbing immaturities which led many of us originally to Jung's psychology. In particular, it is my experience that the fascination and lure of the archetypal world and the temporary lift it gives may tempt us to a premature sense of superiority not fully supported by the basic condition of the personality, and may conceal the underlying and neglected immaturity which is so often the result of early hurts. This is especially likely to occur when, in clear contradiction to the example given by Jung's own heroic endeavour and achievement, we substitute intellectual comprehension for genuine experience. When this happens, it naturally means that this unfaced inferiority is concealed by a power drive, which may itself be masked by pseudo-helplessness or oversensitiveness to prestige, dignity and position.

Jung the teacher

To come back to the earlier days: Jung has been a prodigious worker and he has had available a prodigious volume of energy, both physical and psychical. While in the daytime he worked at his practice with his students and patients, at night he frequently turned this powerful flow of libido inwards, probing into his psyche, thus activating the images there, layer after layer, depth after depth. He said he felt he was in those early days at times on the edge of being overwhelmed. Gradually he learned to safeguard himself in this dangerous work, not to forget those few who were at his side, through whom he could relate to and to whom he could convey some of his inner experiences.

In those days, the late twenties and early thirties, when I first went to Zurich, Jung's seminars, given every Wednesday morning from eleven a.m. to one p.m., with break for coffee and sandwiches, were the event of the week. Jung's capacity as a teacher, not only of the individual but within a group, came out vividly in these seminars. He would take, say, a series of dreams or visions, demonstrating with brilliant flashes of insight not only the individual motifs and their significance for the dreamer but above all their inner sequence and continuity, the dynamic energy pattern of the psyche. This approach he also applied in a masterly analysis of Nietzsche's *Zarathustra*. With a patient unhurriedness, arousing the spirit of discovery in his students and guiding them to find the answers themselves, he emphasised the insight attained rather than the amount of ground covered. Unassuming, with a great big warm-hearted friendliness both in receiving and conveying, he lifted the audience temporarily above themselves. Responding to questions with spontaneous freshness as if it were the first occasion, he would extract relevance from the most unlikely suggestion but firmly maintain the relevant line. On the other hand, Jung spoke to the moment and the particular situation. Hardly anyone attended the seminar without feeling that at some point he was speaking essentially to him or her. He was amazingly 'in Tao'

with the moment and with the students, so that when his spontaneous remarks are retold in another moment of time and in
another context, they may appear absurd, contradictory or even
outrageous.

I think that most people who have met Dr. Jung, particularly
in his later years, feel about him something of the wise old China-
man, the yellow ancestor, with a twinkle in his eye. Personages of
this degree of age and maturity will not tell you what to do in a
particular situation. They are much more likely to tell you a story,
a myth, sometimes even before you have presented any problem,
just after the first exchange of greeting, as if they know instinctively what you have come for. Later you discover how amazingly
apt the story has been, and how in some strange way you are better
able to face your life situation afterwards.

Anima and animus

To come back to the shadow, one of Jung's most important discoveries in it is that of the feminine side in men and the masculine
one in women. He called these dominant centres the anima and the
animus, the soul in a man and the animating spirit in a woman.
Biologically it has for a long time been known that we are made up
of both male and female elements. Jung has helped us to grasp, to
discover and to value the similar situation in our psychological
structure. When we are centred and in harmony with ourselves,
these complementary opposites support us and give us poise and
clearer judgment. But when unrelated, say at loggerheads, intellect against heart, then the stronger of the two will take over and
lead to unsatisfactory, because one-sided, reaction.

As in our bodily state we scarcely know that we have a digestion
until it is upset, or a head until it aches, so in this case it is in the
disturbed condition rather than the positive partnership that we
become first aware of the two. As so often, this is much easier to
see in others than to spot in oneself: the man in a querulous, petty,
irritable mood, his sound judgment blurred, the woman taking an
opinionated stand, knowing everything better, generalising and
out of touch with her natural feminine feeling.

These two forces, male and female, within us were vividly portrayed in a Greek myth recorded by Plato. It says that the original
human was a whole, male and female in one. But when striving to
reach the seat of the gods, the gods got frightened. On their
advice, Zeus, the ruler of the gods, divided the humans into two,
male and female. This diverted their aim, because from then on
each half tried to find its complementary other outside. Jung

saw that the immense misunderstanding lies in the expectation that one can find in an outer woman all the fulfilment a man dreams of and in an outer man all that a woman had hoped to do and to become herself; it means expecting from the other, beyond a good and healthy partnership, what is really the call of one's completion within oneself. Of course, when we are young, we not only hope for but expect this as a natural right. What it really amounts to: if caught too long in such an expectation of finding in the partner what really belongs to oneself, this severely damages any adult relationship, because the partner is not seen as a person in his or her own right, and loved for what he or she are themselves.

Another serious and often most painful misunderstanding derives from the unawareness and lack of appreciation of the fact that, biologically as well as psychologically, we all carry both male and female components. A girl with a good brain, a boy with poetic or artistic leanings may be considered queer by their fellows, and feeling insecure in their own sex may lead them into a false sense of being bluestockings or effeminate, with the hidden fear of being homosexuals.

Becoming aware of, and relating to, the fateful feminine component in man, the anima, and the role of the masculine part in woman, the animus, are thus important stages towards the individual's being able to bring to life his or her full capacity, head and heart, spirit and body.

The opposites and their synthesis

Jung's work is full of growing points, but I think it can be said that they are all related to the basic conception that growth arises from transcending the opposites, of which anima and animus are two of the chief examples. After all, each of our individual lives has stemmed from the original marriage of opposites that took place when the sperm and ovum of our parents united. As mentioned above, Jung has found the psychological counterpart to this biological basis of energy and growth in his fundamental conception of the opposites from which, by including and transcending their tension, we can grow nearer to our potential fulfilment, towards truer wholeness and unity. This is what he called the process of individuation.

Most of his findings can be illuminated and better grasped with the help of this *basic conception of wholeness as a synthesis of opposites*. This concept shines through Jung's demonstration of the compensating role of conscious and unconscious, of light and shadow, through his emphasis on *and* as a synthesis arising from *either/or*. This idea of the creative relationship of the opposites even extends to God *and* Satan. It almost reaches a new dimension in Jung's complementing the vertical function of cause and effect by the horizontal one of meaningful synchronicity.

The self

From his early work on, he has emphasised throughout that the centre of the personality is finally not the ego but a superordinate centre which he called the self, under whose auspices the ego finds its rightful place. This shift of emphasis, reorientation from the ego to a power beyond, might be considered as bringing the picture of the psyche into line with the shift at the end of the Middle Ages from the earth's being the centre of the universe to the discovery that, in reality, the earth is subordinate to the sun.

In his *Job*, Jung assigns to man, the individual, the important part of humanising his relationship to God by man remaining steadfast within the boundaries of his human individuality. Psychologically speaking, this situation of Job somehow mirrors the dynamic relationship between the ego and the divine centre or symbol of wholeness. From a religious point of view and bearing in mind that Jung was not a theologian but a physician who gained his insight from the facts or puzzles observed in his daily clinical experience, one might say that his conception of the self is that of the reflection of the image of God in man.

The religious sense

As a physician and psychiatrist, he had found in his patients and students that at the base of their trouble was their damaged relatedness, or unrelatedness, to the sources of being. Recognising the bearing of their dreams on this calamity led him to his investigation and, finally, to the recovery of religious values which stylised religion had obscured for them. In particular, to those who are not fortunate enough to be held by and belong to an established religious tradition within their community, Jung indeed has something of special value to give. One of his great achievements is that modern man can re-relate to this centre, to the central mystery of one's being, without violating our hard-won rational faculty and experimental approach.

Jung himself lived, as I mentioned before, since his boyhood with the feeling of being under the auspices of something greater than him that called and guided him on his way, that of a pathfinder and mapmaker. All the same, we must understand the human burden he carried in the face of his discoveries and his almost total isolation in his pioneering researches into the so-called irrationalities of the deep unconscious. As would be any other worker in an uncharted field, he was in dire need of confirmation of his findings from independent sources. He found that earlier ages had struggled with the same problems and had observed the basic phenomena before him, though they met them in a different context and, of course, expressed them in the imagery of their own time. This explains his extensive and detailed studies for instance of gnosticism and alchemy.

Jung's impact on our time

To sum up: bringing about the possibility of re-establishing a more conscious relationship with the powers of the unconscious, Jung has immensely widened and deepened the possible scope of human awareness. This relationship between the conscious and the unconscious, on which the health of the expanding human mind depends, he showed in such a way that modern man can accept the realities of those powers without damaging his intellectual integrity.

This development both necessitated and became possible through Jung's epoch-making work of mapping out the structure of the human psyche in modern terms. Hence the significance of his recognition and valuation of the deeper unconscious strata, the collective unconscious, with its clinical and cultural implications, and of his discovery of the dominants of this realm, the archetypes. While to him as a physician the critical test of truth was how it works out in an actual moment of living, in life, yet from his extensive experience and research on a multiplicity of human situations he has reached far beyond and below the individual case, to depths and heights which are common to mankind. The symbols, myths and rites, the fairy tales and folklore which he could thus elucidate are significant for art, education and many a wider aspect of culture. In his interpretation of the symbolism of medieval alchemy he found the process of individuation already foreshadowed.

Counterbalancing the one-sided intellectual development of the last centuries of western civilisation, Jung's work has profoundly influenced not only psychotherapy and psychiatry but also education, art and religious appreciation. From his pioneering investigations and specific discoveries have arisen new attitudes and realisations of great importance to the human individual and society: for example, his discovery, understanding and grasp of the necessity and value of seemingly negative shadow aspects of the personality as potentially constructive; his appreciation of day-dreams and phantasies as messages of the psyche; his development of the technique of relating consciousness to the unconscious through spontaneous forms of expression, for instance in painting, drawing and active imagination; his comprehension of the reality of soul and spirit as expressed in religion and in art, opening a new way of relating to their essential values; his distinction of masculine and feminine features in both men and women, which has lifted a handicapping burden of self-depreciation in both sexes; his recognition and differentiation of the psychological characteristics of women from those of men; his revaluation of the second half of life and its rich specific potentialities, giving meaning to the extension of life made possible by modern medicine; and last but not least, the significance of his findings in regard to nations and civilisations.

Jung the man

Pondering on this life now ended, the image came to me of Jung as a great tree casting its own shadow, lit by many candles, the flame of each radiating an aspect of his rich and varied personality. Their glow gave a luminosity from which each of us, in varying ways, can obtain some manna to feed, to heal and to carry us, and even perhaps to bring hope to an often desperate need. It is for each of us to find at this place of treasure that which rightfully belongs or speaks to us, to each of us according to our readiness, and then to feed it into our own life so as to enliven, to enrich and extend it. In meeting him personally in his seminars in Zurich, and also, not infrequently, when opening one of his books, we were taken out of our egocentricity into a wider, more luminous, numinous, inspired realm and relationship, out of isolation into a realisation of meaning and belongingness, to a realm of significance beyond ourselves. He had a direct relationship with the source of life and being which may well have to do with healing. May we never forget that the insights that arise from both the contemplation of his life and the contents of the volumes he left us, had to be minted by him out of tensions, despair and aloneness that would have daunted or even destroyed a lesser man.

Jung has indeed lived up to his name that, as he himself remarked, literally means 'young'. In reading him it may be difficult to grasp the natural simplicity, unpretentiousness and directness whereby he combined this youngness of spirit with an outstanding maturity. He brought to any subject or occasion, to any person he was speaking to, whether it be a scholar or a peasant in the mountains, a spontaneous freshness and openness. He welcomed any new outlook, discovery, addition to the sum of his knowledge or experience—it might be as controversial as para-psychology—and, eager to greet any contribution to life or thought, was not put off or put out when it required a modification of his established ideas. He never wanted to be the founder of a closed system of psychology or a rigid school. His conception of the psyche includes the *puer aeternus*, the symbol of eternal youth, and Jung's spirit, life and work exemplify what a mature relationship to this divine power may mean.

To see Jung at a learned philosophical meeting was to feel 'Here is the great scholar, the great wise man—perhaps in a former incarnation a member of that group included in the dialogues of Plato.'

Again, to see him cooking a piece of steak and making a subtle sauce for it, over the fire he had lit in his stone hideout, partly built by his own hands, at the upper end of the Lake of Zurich near the mountains, to see him reach down into a hole in the ground and take out a bottle of carefully chosen wine, to par-take of this simple hand-made yet almost ritual-like meal with him, was to feel, 'Here is a peasant of the country who in his way is an aristocrat, an aristocrat of the soil.'

To see him at a festive party or at a carnival ball, to hear his Rabelaisian stories and wit, to see the way he included personally every member of the party, was to feel 'Surely here is someone who belongs to the ancient and royal order of Bacchus or Dionysus, who has come amongst us once again.'

At the end of one of my longer periods at Zurich, I was ponder-ing on what had impressed me most about Jung. I felt that some-how it was not only his learning, great as it was, not only his deep insight into the subleties and depths of the human psyche. No! There seemed to be, I felt, something beyond all this, something that held and carried his spirit. Then it suddenly flashed in on me, not these alone, something more: it was his humanness.

II

The Psychiatric Field

II

EARLY WORK IN AN OBSERVATION WARD

(a) A RECOLLECTION (1966)

Between 1929 and 1935 I was privileged to pioneer an out-patient clinic attached to the observation ward in Whitechapel of which I was the assistant medical officer in charge. In those days, patients admitted to an observation ward were sorted out, either to be certified and then sent on to a mental institution, wherever a bed was available, or else to be discharged to where they came from, no treatment or after-care being available. A psychotherapeutic approach to so-called mental cases had scarcely been considered yet, neither had to any extent the interrelationship between physical symptoms and the psychological condition. It was in this situation that I decided to improvise a psychotherapeutic out-patient clinic (on the quiet).

My patients were drawn from two sources: those who came in under temporary certificates but who although not requiring to be sent on to a mental hospital, I felt could benefit from psychotherapy such as could be given in an out-patient setting, and those who came to the hospital for general medical help, from toothache to anxiety complaints. When I was 'on the door', that is, on admission, I was able to select and appropriate, if I may say so, some valuable 'cases' which did not require admission but later revealed rich psychotherapeutic material.

No facilities were available for this work. It was both unofficial and, in a way, illegitimate, i.e. it was quite unsanctioned and not without risk to one's reputation. To be engaged in activities outside the hospital routine such as talking tête-à-tête to an ex-lady patient seated, with our back to the gangway, in the corridor joining the main hall to the midwifery ward, the quietest place available, was considered somewhat strange and even suspicious.

Almost exactly thirty years ago I read a paper to the Analytical Psychology Club on some of the results of this work in what one might rightfully call the first Jungian Clinic in London, probably in England. It was in this pioneering work that I first really experienced the value of a sequence of dreams following the trail of the anima, and the potency of spontaneous pictures, sometimes alarmingly so.* Out of the experience of those times, using the insights and especially the pattern and dynamics of the psyche as developed by Jung, I gradually found the way to my own contribution which led to the conception of the critical hurt and healing in depth, and the crucial significance of what I have called the feed-back.

(b) PSYCHOTHERAPY IN THE OBSERVATION WARD (1935)

It has always seemed to me that the observation wards, instead of being used merely for preliminary diagnosis and as clearing houses prior to disposal, might become centres for psychotherapy and, indirectly, educational centres for the general public in matters of mental health. Five years' experience as a medical officer in observation wards which dealt with about six hundred cases a year, confirmed me in the belief that this is not an idle phantasy, but something which can be translated into actual practice. Even though special circumstances limit the amount that can be accomplished, it is nevertheless necessary to have these aims clearly defined, if the observation ward is to develop along the lines indicated by its unique position in the mental health service of the community.

I want to sketch briefly for you some of the opportunities I have found there for psychotherapy.

The arrival

We will commence with the arrival of the patient. Here at the beginning is a situation which often requires considerable psychological judgment. Not infrequently an otherwise quiet patient becomes resistive and violent at the moment of entry, and we find that the relatives have thought it necessary to deceive him as to his destination so that he would accompany them quietly. He arrives, not as he had expected at the convalescent home, the post office or (as in one case) the night-club, but at a place which

*See the case histories presented below in 'Some Notes on Jung's Contribution to Psychiatry'.

savours suspiciously of the unknown and confirms his idea that his relatives are trying to 'put him away'. Or the newly-admitted patient may protest: '*I* am not mad; all *these* people are mad,' and this may not be quite untrue.

It is surprising how often in these difficult situations the alarm or distress of the patient can be allayed by the medical officer establishing an appropriate relationship with him, so that he has the person in authority standing with him and no longer needs to meet his inner terrors alone. He feels 'accepted', and that sense of isolation which is so often a part of the burden of the patient is relieved.

This is the critical time in relation to the family as well. The relatives often arrive at the hospital in a state of greater agitation than the patient. Upon more than one occasion on the arrival of the family party at the hospital door I have mistaken another member of the family for the patient.

It is essential to secure the family's co-operation from the start. A relative offended inadvertently on the doorstep may refuse to co-operate and later may even actively interfere with the treatment, his negative or even hostile attitude being conveyed to the patient. It is important to remember that usually this is the first time the relatives have been in a mental ward and know nothing of its procedure. Added to this they may be exhausted and irritable from days, weeks or even months of a heroic struggle to keep the son, wife or daughter from being sent away to the 'mad-house', there, as they believe, to be 'put away for the rest of his life'.

This is no exaggeration. The general idea of a mental hospital is usually that of a lunatic asylum such as existed a hundred years ago. Their imagination has been fed by lurid tales handed down from grandparents and parents, and kept alive by an occasional lurid story in the sensational press. The terrified exclamation: 'If I let my boy go to the mad-house, they will keep him there for ever,' is not an uncommon one. 'I know I am signing his death warrant, but I have done all I can to keep him at home,' said one mother when signing the application form for admission of her son to a mental hospital.

These generations-old, and at one time only too well-founded, prejudices are very difficult to eradicate. But to my mind it is of extreme importance to correct such ideas both in the minds of patients and relatives, and through them the general public. It takes time when one feels it can ill be spared and patience which seems unnatural unless one appreciates the reasons for such hostility and stubbornness.

Relations and friends need to learn that mental illness is an illness just as much as scarlet fever or tuberculosis; that each requires treatment away from home in a special hospital; that each requires that it be 'certified' (that terrible word) that the patient is suffering from the illness which the special hospital treats; and above all, that in each the aim of the hospital is to get the patient well in the shortest possible space of time and so send him home and make room for one more on the long waiting list.

Psychotherapy for the relatives

Every patient is to some degree identified with the members of his immediate family and they with him. For practical purposes, therefore, I look upon the family as extensions of the patient and take the time to listen to their problems and talk with them about them. This one does of course not only at the time the patient is admitted but also as necessary from time to time throughout the whole period of treatment. Frequently, personal problems which directly influence the patient's illness come to light and are dealt with. Sometimes, indeed, though the patient himself is at the time too deeply engulfed by his illness to be accessible to psychotherapy, one finds a relative who is on the verge of a nervous breakdown and in urgent need of help. In such a case I think it lies within the province of the medical officer to give what help he can, or is able to find time for, according to the urgency, even though the relative is not officially a patient.

Occasionally a relative will ask for permission to attend as an out-patient, or an out-patient will bring a relative in for consultation. Sometimes it seems advisable to keep in touch with an entire family. One such case is that of Mrs. W.B., whose husband was once a patient and who later had disappeared from home and had not been heard of since. There are two bright boys, five- and eight-years-old. The psychiatric social worker has kept in close touch with the family, and both the wife and children are seen by me occasionally. We are attempting to lessen the feeling of insecurity and incompleteness which threatened at one time seriously to involve the whole family, because of the suspense and uncertainty about the father.

I just referred to the necessity of securing the relatives' co-operation in treating the patient. Often the lack of it is due to ignorance. Sometimes changing the attitude of the family towards the patient and his illness is a more difficult problem of education than that of the patient himself. In the case of R.T., a young man in a state of almost complete dissociation, the parents alternately wept over him and urged him to 'pull himself together', while a brother who was a policeman gave more drastic advice, even threatening to 'beat sense into' him. It is easy to imagine the difficult time this patient must have had on his return from the mental hospital.

At the other extreme we find the insight and co-operation of the husband of Mrs. S.P. He himself was on the verge of a nervous breakdown and suffered intensely from his wife's behaviour during her illness. However, he worked with me on his problems concurrently with his wife's treatment and thus was able to wait more or less patiently for the favourable development which ultimately took place in her.

The handling of the relatives often requires as much psychological insight and skill as the treatment of the patient. One of my early failures in this connection was with the husband of Mrs. E.T. The patient recovered sufficiently to be discharged after a few days, but her condition demanded intensive psychotherapy over many months. Insufficient contact had been established with her husband during the acute stage of her illness when he was thoroughly alarmed about her condition. After she returned home he became antagonistic to the idea of further treatment. For a time this interfered seriously with her progress, but fortunately I was able later to gain his co-operation, and with this there was an immediate improvement in the patient.

There is no need for me to emphasise further the importance of including the family in one's consideration of the patient. But before I leave them altogether, I must say that always at the back of my mind there was the thought that it is through relatives and others associated with the patient that erroneous ideas concerning mental hospitals can be corrected; and that perhaps in time a new attitude will spread to the general public and that they will have some appreciation of the hospital facilities available, and the value of early recognition and treatment of mental illness.

Social background and after-care

Now to get back to the patient. In nearly every case the psychiatric social worker visits his or her home and place of work and obtains as complete a social history as possible. Such a history gives the medical officer a good background for his picture of the case. His task is to bring together all the relevant data from the social worker, from the story told by the relatives, from the patient's own account, from his and the nurses' observation of the patient, and from his interpretation of the dream and phantasy material disclosed to him by the patient. He must then decide what is the best line of procedure in this particular case – whether the patient should be sent to a mental hospital or to a general ward, or be discharged home; and if the latter, whether he should have intensive psychotherapy as an out-patient.

The records show that about half the number of patients which come into an observation ward are transferred for treatment to mental hospitals. Of the remainder, a small number go to general wards, but the majority are discharged in care of their relatives.

After he or she leaves the observation ward or the mental hospital, the patient still has to face the problem that caused his or her admission, and the important task is to prevent a relapse by helping him to deal with the factors that precipitated the breakdown. Besides, it is worth considering that a nervous breakdown need not be an entirely negative happening. It is often a great revealer of the extent of the distortion of the individual from his natural pattern. On the other hand, it may give him a great opportunity and become an incentive which otherwise he might never have had to correct that distortion and to develop a way of life more in harmony with his individual nature.

With this in mind it has been my practice to ask each patient at the time of discharge to let me know from time to time how he was getting on, and I invited him to write or telephone for an appointment and come in to see me if he thought I could be of help to him. If he seemed suitable for intensive psychotherapy, he came up regularly for treatment as often as his situation demanded (or as my time would allow), but in most cases what one might call psychological supervision was all that was possible or advisable.

When a patient went on to a mental hospital, I invited the family at the time of transfer to bring him in when he was discharged. Several such patients came up at regular intervals or at such times as they felt the menace of their problems once again. It is obvious that it is advantageous to lay the foundation for such prophylactic after-care as early as possible. As I have already indicated, every effort is made to establish a good relationship with the patient and his family while he is still in the observation ward, so that he will be willing to come back later, if necessary.

One reason for keeping in touch with these patients myself is that the provision for after-care in London is at present (1936) inadequate. Furthermore, I believe that a patient does better when he continues to work with the psychotherapist who made the initial contact with him and who already knows him and his home and work environment.

Another reason why it seems to me advisable for such patients

to continue to work psychologically with the officer attached
to the observation ward rather than be referred to an independent
psychological clinic, is that these clinics often have long waiting
lists and the patient may have to wait for months before he can
obtain the help he needs.

How far is psychotherapy worth while?

Mental hospitals are usually unable to treat the patient psychologically owing to the enormous numbers of patients in proportion to medical officers. The deputy medical superintendent of a
mental hospital told me that in the last few weeks he had admitted
several patients who obviously would have benefited by intensive
psychotherapy, but there was no one to whom he could refer them
and that he himself had no time available.

Whether it is financially worth while to give to individual
patients the many hours necessary for psychotherapy is sometimes
questioned. In my opinion the point at which economy should be
practised is in the initial selection of cases. This selection requires
much care. One needs to take into consideration (1) the patient's
past history evaluated in relation to his environment; (2) the
actual load, often much greater than the apparent load, under
which he has broken down; (3) his intelligence; and (4) what for
want of a better term I call 'moral fibre'. Finally, the psychiatrist's
intuition, checked on knowledge gained from previous experience,
will also have its part to play.

Although the number suited for deep therapy is small, my
experience indicates that these individuals are highly valuable
psychologically and are well worth the time and effort expended
in helping them to develop sufficient maturity so that they themselves can deal satisfactorily with their problems and lead a
worthwhile life.

SOME NOTES ON JUNG'S CONTRIBUTION TO PSYCHIATRY (1966)

Jung's contribution to psychiatry, as I see it, is three-fold. First,
in my experience his concepts of the structure of the psyche* can
be of basic importance in the understanding of mental disorder.
Second, the psychiatrist's grasp, enriched and deepened by these
concepts, and the attitude which it may bring about towards the
patient and his illness, can (in favourable cases) help to build up

*Described in some detail in 'C. G. Jung, The Man and his Work' (see above,
pp. 15–35).

a human relationship which I have experienced as a healing factor in the treatment of mental illness. Lastly, Jung's approach is to take even the most irrational-sounding fixed ideas or stereotyped movements as potentially meaningful, if only we, the physicians, can gain a glimpse of insight into their origin and significance. This seems to me of great importance as a guiding principle.

In the case histories that follow, I shall try to illustrate some aspects of the structure of the psyche as well as the attitude of the psychiatrist, while for the last point I will quote an experience of Jung himself.

Jung's probing into the collective unconscious and the world of the archetypes has acquainted us with the irrational and its power and helped us to get related to it consciously, a fact of great importance I found when trying to follow and contact the mentally ill patient, overwhelmed as he is by just such forces.

The insight and experience of the great powers which we very clearly see welling up in a psychosis and find in a less threatening form (potentially) in the psyche of everyone, enable a therapist with this approach to make contact with these negatively experienced powers of the patient and give him a chance to take the patient out of his isolation which is certainly one of the most painful aspects of his suffering. Jung's discovery of what he called the collective unconscious in which he found such basic powers, may be of help to the physician, if he knows of them himself. By this, I do not mean to say that we need to have a psychosis to get a relationship to psychotic patients. But by his own contact with the collective unconscious the physician, as a human being, naturally has these forces potentially within himself.

In the psychotic state, the ego of the individual is threatened and overwhelmed for shorter or longer periods by one or several autonomous powers of the collective unconscious, and even his most wonderful dreams go over him like waves and cannot heal or guide him, because there is no ego that could relate them constructively to the reality of the moment—most likely, Rosen,* often so successful in treating schizophrenics, tried to stand in as his ill patient's ego till the patient could gradually take over.

Possession by an archetype

I would like to give now an example of 'clear-cut' possession by an archetype. It was that of a patient I had many years ago, a man

*John N. Rosen (*Direct Analysis*, Gruner & Stratton, New York, 1953) showed that, under favourable conditions, psychotherapeutic treatment of hospitalised schizophrenic patients was possible. (*Ed.*)

of about thirty. He was walking down the city street when, one afternoon, he suddenly heard the words of divine command: 'Be fruitful and multiply, and replenish the earth!' The mental hospital ward I worked at was half a mile down the road, and a little later this man was brought in by a policeman, evidently having proceeded at once to invite feminine partners to help him fulfil the divinely appointed task. On examining him, I found him physically in good health and a likeable man, quiet and of humble demeanour, and the seriousness of his conviction deeply impressed me. I tried to show him the reality and consequences involved in the literal carrying out of his mission, but I soon found that he was completely possessed by this basic creative power and that the ego was overwhelmed, and as then there was no provision for long-term observation, he had to be sent to a mental hospital. I regret this, knowing from later work with patients in a psychotic phase that if I can be present at a moment of emergence, and with the knowledge and appreciation of these archetypal forces, I may, in acknowledging the profound inner experience, be able to relate to the just-emerging ego and (if one might say so) in compassion strengthen it, so that even though he cannot be held just then, I might have a better chance next time. Because this man was overwhelmed by what we might call the God of creativity, one would look into his earlier development to see where this basic power had not been given the appropriate acknowledgment and consideration, as for instance in a repressive puritanical environment, in this so severe case probably of more than one generation.

A psychotic breakdown and its positive effects

A little later, with another patient, Miss K.Y., I did have the opportunity to follow up a psychotic, an overwhelmed patient. I met in her a striking example of what seems to amount to a tendency of the unconscious to correct an adaptation that is on too restricted a base. She was an intelligent young woman with a colourful personality whose work for ten years had been the mechanical task of folding paper boxes in a factory which in no way made use of her creative imagination or of her basic intelligence. Her personal life was equally narrow and she lived largely in phantasy.

She was sent in to the observation ward where I was at that time the medical officer. She was brought in by the police, in a state of acute dissociation, and thus not accessible to psychological treatment. Her story was that during her lunch hour she had yielded to an irresistible impulse and climbed into the front seat of a large motor-car, probably a Rolls-Royce, that was waiting outside the Mansion House, the residence of the Lord Mayor of London; she sat down alongside the chauffeur, apparently in a friendly spontaneous manner but which was quite irrational under the circumstances. As it became obvious that she was out of contact with outer reality, she was a little later admitted to the observation ward, which once again was conveniently just down the road! She was very excited and among other things imagined she was engaged to Prince George (the late Duke of Kent). When I saw her next morning, she seemed quite sensible, however, and told me in detail and with much apparent insight the origin of her illness: how a few months previously, while on holiday, she had gone to a dance given in honour of a warship visiting a seaside town. The glamour of this naval ball greatly thrilled her, and she reproached herself for having been too timid to allow one of her partners to see her home even though chaperoned by a girl friend.

She was caught up by the idea of the Royal Navy and its sailors. When she returned home from her holiday, she wrote to a newspaper saying what a shame it was that certain hotels and resorts in seaside towns prohibited sailors from entering their doors. She championed their cause, saying this was an unjust slur on them, that they were really splendid and well-behaved.

The letter was printed in the newpaper, and to her surprise she had many letters from sailors and even petty officers thanking her. She continued correspondence with some, and one she had actually met and taken to her home when he was on leave. She was still in correspondence with another, and they both wrote affectionately to each other every week, neither of them ever having seen the other.

She thought all this excitement had caused her breakdown. I said to myself: 'What remarkable insight. This girl will soon be well again.' But as a parting shot I said to her: 'Have you ever seen that sailor again—the one you took home?'

'No,' she answered. 'But I have seen his picture.'

Smelling a rat, I asked, 'Where?' and she replied: 'In the *Sunday Express* this morning.'

My suspicions being confirmed, I then asked: 'Who was he?' and she replied: 'The Prince of Wales. Wasn't that lovely?' I said: 'It certainly was,' and we shook hands. I was also told that later that day she entertained the ward by taking off her clothes and doing what she thought was a cabaret act.

She was transferred to a mental hospital where for several

weeks her life hung in the balance: she was critically ill, had to be tube-fed for six weeks. Her conscious relation to her environment was obliterated, and for several months nurses became a necessary substitute for her submerged ego. Gradually she came out of her delirium and eventually, after three or four months, was discharged home. Her mother brought her to see me. By that time, my work in the observation ward having come to an end, I saw her privately over several years once or twice a week for psychotherapy. During these sessions she told me that she remembered the conversation with me in the observation ward, where obviously a link was made with me, in actual reality. I have often wondered whether my listening to her and grasping, though ever so vaguely, the deep significance of her phantasy life, had held her as if by a thread of human relationship on her perilous voyage through the underworld of her psychosis. Gradually she could also remember some of her inner experiences during her stay in the mental hospital. She said: 'In my delirium I lived through the ages; the time of Christ; the time of Nero; at one time I thought I was the Madonna, then Helen of Troy' — the most beautiful woman on earth.

Silently translating to myself these images, which one could so easily debunk as plain nonsense, I recognised them as the imagery of powerful aspects of basic instincts, in short what Jung calls archetypes of the collective unconscious. Feeling, indeed with some awe, their significance, I was able to truthfully decrease her own fear of madness and thus alleviate her burden of shame and humiliation of having been in a mental hospital, a reaction to a damaging prejudice which one still has to deal with despite all the efforts made to decrease the stigma.

Before, however, I attempted to canalise her newly freed energies and sense of meaning and lead them into our world of reality, these powerful realisations of her potential self had to undergo a humanising transition. I recall, for instance, a colourful dream of hers of a gipsy girl dancing with a natural joy of movement and freedom. This was half-way between the suppressed natural woman doing a frenzied dance in the observation ward, out of control, and the attractive and beautiful image of Helen of Troy, the ideal of femininity in antiquity and still being portrayed and reproduced on the screen. The gipsy, though on the fringe of our social pattern, can be met in the Here and Now, and thus the dream could be understood as a link with our patient's natural self between extremes of self-abandon.

It almost seems as if it needed a psychotic breakdown to activate her potential self and to bring up her basic instinctual powers so that they might be blended into the possibilities and limitations of our accepted social setting. During her analysis she grew to develop those sides of herself which had formerly been buried in the unconscious, but she also learned to live them in her every-day life. As I said before, her work in the factory had been quite an inadequate expression of her personality, and necessarily she had to look elsewhere for intellectual and emotional satisfaction.

She started by attending evening classes. After some time, she got a scholarship to a residential training college and eventually became a competent psychiatric social worker. As such she was appointed to a rehabilitation centre for officer ex-prisoners of war and in her personal life could form some friendships — an impor-tant step in weaning her from what had been at times a very heavy transference on me. To give you an idea of it: I still remember her mother calling on me one day and asking in a friendly way whether it was really true that I was going to marry her daughter!

Eventually she became a county child care officer. The experiences she had passed through and what may be called their integration in analysis must have enabled her to do her work in a specially understanding way. As just one example, at the later stages of her work with me she arrived one day with a large bundle under her arm. On being asked, she said it contained boys' clothes which she had to bring later in the day to a child who, after living for six years as a little girl, had just been declared a boy — what a job to do and do it well! It certainly appears that rather than being weakened, she had drawn strength and humanity from the fear-some journey through her illness and the encounter with the archetypal powers.

Some years later Miss K.Y. could enter into a meaningful love relationship with a professional man and even fulfil a long-held wish of hers to buy with her savings a small house of her own with a garden. I am sorry to say that, unfortunately, at the height of her career she died of a cerebral hæmorrhage.

In these two situations we have found first the man overwhelmed by the power of male creativity and then the young woman who had to go through the experience of primitive sexuality, erupting in an archaic form but spanning even to Helen of Troy, the ideal image of womanly beauty. In both instances, the insight into the significance and range of the archetypal forces supported the psychiatrist in grasping that somewhere there was sense in the nonsense, and so gave him a better chance to establish a healing relationship with the patient.

The tracing of the anima

In the third example, a more direct application of an analytical therapeutic approach could help disentangle and sort out what seemed in the beginning a completely fixed and crazy situation. The last of these three mentally disturbed patients shows more clearly the inner psychological structure of a 'normal' man, and the development of his illness reflects it with unusual clarity. Treatment included the tracing of what Jung has called the anima, man's feminine inner counterpart, a power which, if taken in the wrong way, may render his life a misery or become a dangerous experience of infatuation, but if comprehended in the right way, can lead him towards a more meaningful and fulfilled life.

The patient was an intelligent unmarried Jewish man of thirty-three. Eighteen months before he came under my care he had had some teeth extracted and a partial denture fitted. His complaint was that since this dental treatment was done he felt unable to eat properly, because his 'back teeth closed before his front teeth'. He had the most extraordinary feeling about this, and while telling me about it, he bit fiercely on a pencil, clenching his hands in agony to show what the feeling was like. He had gradually lost the ability to work and could no longer keep a job, although he had formerly had a good income. He insisted that the difficulty with his teeth had caused him to lose fluency in speech, undermined his health, prevented him from working and made him sexually impotent.

He was encouraged to talk freely about himself and to pay attention to what he dreamed. Although deeply engrossed with the problem of his teeth, he talked at length of his former sexual exploits. He was accustomed to have sexual relations with a woman once in three or four months but would have seven or eight orgasms in that night. Eventually he had sought out a woman for this purpose and to his intense humiliation discovered that he was impotent. He had not been with a woman since.

After a month of treatment he started to recollect dreams, and soon a whole series emerged which in time led us to the source of his present trouble. He had formed a positive relationship to me, so that I could risk to interpret at times. Up to then, his insistence was absolute that his teeth were the cause of all his difficulties, and he was sincerely surprised when I tentatively suggested that, in view of his sexual habits and now of his impotence, they might be related to a sexual problem.

First dream: 'I have stabbed a man about fifty years old.' He now remembered that he had had a similar dream several months earlier when he had said to the man as he stabbed him: 'An eye for an eye and a tooth for a tooth.'

Second dream, the following night: 'A fair-haired nun with blue eyes came towards me and said: "Don't you recognise me?" I replied: "Of course I do, May." Then she wanted to give me a coin like a shilling; only it was not a shilling, it was a sort of charm. She explained that it would bring me success and happiness. I said: "It is more than I dare to do." I felt that I must not take it, and I was upset that I had to refuse it. Then I awoke.'

This dream stirred him deeply. He told me that May was a girl whom he had met at the age of eighteen while he was in camp at Plymouth during the last war. They met only three times, although they were deeply attracted to each other. Because she was a Roman Catholic he decided to break off the relationship, for he felt that she was so fine and sensitive that she could not accept the Jewish religion without great spiritual injury to herself, and he was not ready to do her that injury. He said: 'I had a spiritual feeling for her; it was not lust.' Perhaps her present was the Queen's Shilling which used to be a binding token of the acceptance of enlistment in the service of the Queen.

Six years later he had gone to Plymouth for his holidays in order to seek information about her, and learned that she had married and subsequently died in childbirth. He was deeply affected and immediately returned to London.

He told me that after giving up this girl he had never allowed himself to get to know fair-haired girls, always going with brunettes. He never felt 'spiritual' towards brunettes, he said, only physical and rather vicious. For instance, he would tease a brunette until, to use his words, she was 'white-hot' and then say he did not want her. But he had stopped this since one had violently resented it and stabbed him with a pair of scissors.

Two days later (i.e. after the fair-haired nun dream) —

Third dream: 'I dreamed that I was in a warm place. There were crocodiles and pythons. I thought: "It is funny they do not attack anyone. Maybe the heat is not strong enough to make them alive." Suddenly you [referring to me] got a cane and hit one of them on the head. It made a dive for me, and just as it was about to leap, its head fell off and I walked out.'

The dream shows that we are on dangerous ground, but since the outcome is positive, it seemed safe to go ahead, though with special care.

A few days after this dream he saw a religious film *The White Sister*. He was not interested until a nun appeared, and then he followed with emotion and close attention. There was also a military scene which reminded him of Plymouth. That same night he dreamed:

Fourth dream: 'I am in the room where I waited for you, Dr. Barker, last time. You come in and ask: "Have you had any dreams?" At first I say "No", and then I remember the dream in which I killed someone. I tell you that I remember that his name was M.F., the dentist I had all the trouble with.'

We remember the first dream in which the patient had stabbed a man of fifty. Now, a fortnight later, in a dream within a dream, as though twice removed from his everyday life and reaching deeper layers, suggesting a more co-operative relationship with the unconscious, the name of the man he had murdered came up and he could hold it — that of his dentist.

Then he remembered that two days after he said goodbye to May, the girl in Plymouth, he had met a man who made an insulting remark of a sexual nature about her. This man looked like the dentist, M.F. He had wanted to fight the man, but a dark girl who was present separated them, and as she walked away with the patient she said to him: 'Why fight? No girl is a maid.' Although this made him very angry, he felt he could not strike her because she was a woman. When we discussed the dream, he said: 'Now I know why I tease brunettes; I am hitting back at them because I could not hit the dark girl who said "No girl is a maid." '

To look more closely at the dreams, the first states plainly that he has murdered a man, and thus is a murderer. I, the analyst, accepted this without passing judgment or recrimination. Taking the dream as reflecting an Oedipal situation, the patient's dilemma being stated as clearly as this, we could conclude that he is ready for deep analysis.

In the second dream, a fair-haired woman asks whether he does not recognise her, and he says: 'Of course I do, May' — the name of his sweetheart, fifteen years or more ago. But the dream makes it quite clear that May is a nun and, as such, an untouchable virgin — possibly also linking her up with the early mother image. The present she offers him, a token of belongingness that would bring him success and happiness — this present, to his utter regret, he must not accept. Is it because, deep down, he also feels that, as a murderer, he is unworthy of it?

In the third dream, however, Dr. Barker not only has a cane but dares to use it: he hits the dangerous creature on the head, which falls off. Taking the head not only as a phallic sign but indicating the negative animus and the whole 'devouring animal' as perhaps a negative mother figure, the physician's blow certainly helped to depotentiate a psychological pattern including the concept that one must not hit a woman or even be aggressive at all. Although a known person appearing as a dream figure may well be taken first as, and associated on, the actual person, it is also often helpful to follow this up by regarding the figure as an emerging undeveloped potential or repressed aspect of the dreamer himself. His physician, in this respect, has become a man, a positive father, so much needed to free the son from the mother ties. We know from the dream that the patient felt the dangerous animals to be quiet because it was not hot enough, and when 'Dr. Barker' hit one of them on the head (thus stirring it up and raising the heat, we wonder?) the creature dived for him, the dreamer; he must have expected to be attacked, to be punished. When mother-fixated, he is still within babyhood, but father's showing that mother is a very fallible creature and not almighty, releases his libido from his first love object and sets him free—he walks out.

The fourth dream shows that we are on the right track in our understanding. In the presence of 'Dr. Barker' who cares for his dreams, the patient not only recalls the act of killing but even the initials of the person he so hated that he wanted to kill him, the dentist. In the association to the dream, however, it came out that the dentist is only a pointer to the man he really wanted to kill—the man who had abused May fifteen years before in Plymouth. If we recall that all the patient's complaints, to be unable to eat properly, to hold a job, to have sexual intercourse, were related to the dentist, it is rather remarkable that he merely reflected the original offender who had deprecated the purity of his great love, whoever this girl was in the last resort. Therefore we have to ask why this could have hurt him so deeply and cause such severe symptoms.

We wonder how a person he only met three times and who, we must not forget, appeared in his dream as a nun, could have exerted such an impact. We remember in this context that the feminine potential which every man carries within him, which Jung called the anima, is the counterpart to his maleness and becomes activated by an outer feminine figure. This knowledge of what we might call the anatomy and physiology of the male psyche prompted me to carefully scan the experiences of the patient's earlier years to see whether there was a trail that led up to this image.

As our analytical work developed, I could eventually discover the imagery that reflected his inner feminine side, and finally track it down as far as his school days. The birth of the anima occurred when, between ten and twelve, he saw a picture of St. George and the dragon, the hero rescuing a fair-haired damsel from the beast. She evidently evoked and reflected his dawn woman. Soon after this, he told me, he became attracted to a young fair-haired girl at school, went round with her, paid her his attentions and fought the bully of the school on her behalf. The picture of St. George rescuing the fair maiden from the dragon came alive in the reality of the boy's experience with the fair-haired girl and the bully. Thus, I could understand that when he met the fair-haired May as a young man, she had an impelling fascination for him because, once again, she personified and activated his individual feminine centre, as different from the infantile fixation on the biological mother. Corresponding so well to the inner image of his anima, she had to be a maiden and he, as St. George, had to fight on her behalf. As we remember, he was indeed ready to fight the man who made a disparaging remark about May, but was prevented from acting according to his inner ideal and natural feeling by the dark-haired girl who had added insult to injury with her remark 'No girl is a maid.' Prevented by collective standards of behaviour from hitting this woman, he suffered a rebound of his vital energy inwards. Throughout subsequent years, he still acted out his revenge on brunettes, which at the same time kept him related vicariously to his fair-haired maiden, though in a very unhappy way. We can understand now the words 'An eye for an eye and a tooth for a tooth', this archaic expression of primitive justice, when in his earlier dream he had killed the man. The dentist, so many years later, not only reminded him of this person but actually took his teeth out, and to his dismay he could once more not hit back—which actually rendered him 'impotent' with regard to speech, work and sex. This shows to what instinctual and early beginnings this trauma probably extended. The intensity of his affect, in which both the male and the female components were involved, makes one naturally link it back to a child's experience of the parental relationship—whatever this may have been which one would like to explore at an appropriate time.

In parenthesis, it might be added that the analyst, when hitting the dangerous creature on the head in the third dream, had as it were taken the place of St. George in the patient's boyhood picture, who by slaying the 'dragon' freed the fair-haired damsel, his anima.

A spectacular change took place when we had reached this phase in his treatment. His life feeling, his vitality returned. He was freed from his immobilisation. He had regained the energy which had been fixed in the complex of obsession about his teeth. The patient was filled with enthusiasm, eager to get a job and, as he said, marry and settle down. The fact that he could consider marriage suggests that by the treatment the archetypal mother fixation was sufficiently resolved and that through the positive relationship to his analyst he had experienced a father who actively took his side.

I am still sorry that at this point of his recovery my work necessitated leaving the hospital. However, he took his discharge happily, having regained his contact with outer reality. I personally would have thought that he would have needed a continuity of deep therapy for a considerable time, in order to lessen the tension between the fair-haired nun, too sacred and holy to be touched by man, and the earthy dark woman as the partner of his most lustful sexuality. Although we know from experience that such a division of the inner woman is quite common, this man evidently had a rare degree of integrity which had not allowed him to live his life in this divided way. Without doubt sooner or later he would meet the dark or the light one again, which would constellate once more this basic problem, but with his newly won insight and if given appropriate support at such critical moments, he might have a chance for another step towards further maturity and fuller integration.

Personally speaking, this trailing of the anima and her Protean disguises and devious ways opened my eyes and alerted my mind to many other occasions when my work called me to track down to their origin this and other basic powers of life.

Meaningful fixed ideas

As an example of the potential meaningfulness of irrational fixed ideas or stereotyped movements, I think of Jung's own experience* with a chronic case in the Burghölzli, the famous mental hospital of Zurich. It was an old lady who had been there for several decades. She more or less continuously occupied herself with strange movements of her hands which nobody could explain. Jung became rather intrigued by these movements and asked the oldest nurse who had known the patient soon after admission as a young woman; she recalled that it was said that the patient had been engaged to a village shoemaker, and just before the wedding he had gone off with another girl. With

*C. G. Jung, Collected Works, Vol. 3, para. 358; Memories, Dreams, Reflections, p. 125.

this information Jung recognised the movements her hands were making as those of a shoemaker with his characteristic way of sewing and pulling out the double thread in a two-handed pull. This movement thus led back to the beginning of her illness, and Jung thought that, if this had been understood earlier, there might have been a chance to link up with what her fiancé had meant to her, support her at the moment of shock and disaster and bring her back into everyday life.

III

Problems of Psychotherapy

III

SOME POSITIVE VALUES OF NEUROSIS (1947)

The problem of neurosis is one that few people can ignore at the present time. The whole world is in a state of unrest. What for generations, for centuries, have been civilised cultural dwelling places are showing cracks and instability in foundations, walls and roofs. Where we once found security, encouragement and rooted-ness, we now find doubt, cynicism and uncertainty. It is inevitable that the universal turmoil should have its counterpart within the individual psyche and vice versa. The individual is a unit within the larger group in which he lives and his unconscious intermingles with the conscious collective. No one can be separated from the times in which he lives. There is no homestead in the land so secluded that it can escape the wild winds that are now blowing.

These are days in which the traditional standards of our fathers no longer meet our deep and tangled problems. We now need that deeper wisdom which lies concealed beyond and below conscious-ness – wisdom which in former days was more satisfactorily mediated by tradition and religious rituals. Previously the roots of our being remained steady in the depths, even though the boughs swayed and tossed above. Now we begin to feel that fear-making loosening of roots. It is not too much to say that every institution, every individual is now faced with the challenge 'Look to your foundation.' It is there that we might find a new insight into the original necessity out of which our institutions and traditions grew.

Problems of good and evil, God and Devil could in former days usually be dealt with in customary ways, often by pious admoni-tions. Now this does not suffice, and we find it imperative to look into things previously avoided as unwholesome or even unclean. 'Get thee behind me, Satan' – meaning 'Get you back into the unconscious' – is no longer effective.

Likewise, neurosis cannot just be dismissed with depreciatory terms. 'Neurosis' and 'nuisance' are words readily coupled together. The person with a neurosis *is* a nuisance, a nuisance to himself and to others. But where there is neurosis, there is energy and value which are demanding to be made conscious: neurosis indicates repressed values. It can be understood as a natural reaction of the total personality to the rejection of qualities essential to life and consciousness. Such repressed values, if attached to other contents of the unconscious, form a complex which often can express itself only through so-called neurotic symptoms. One can say that a neurosis indicates that the personality is striving for healing, towards wholeness. It is my conviction that a healing power lies hidden in neurosis and that it contains the means of restoring lost or rejected values to healthy participation in the life of the individual.

In order to appreciate the structure of this illness, it is necessary to have a picture of the healthy development of the individual.

Every person contains within himself at birth all the latent capacities which are available for use throughout his life. For instance, it is already determined at the time of conception whether he will be tall and lean, or short and stocky. He is born with an inherent personal pattern of his own individual potentialities which contains the vital impulse, the energy to grow and develop and accomplish his life's task. It is as though this pattern were a living mosaic, each stone of which is charged with energy assigned to a particular aspect of life. Can one say, we are meant to live and grow and work towards a more complete expression that arises out of our energy pattern, within the framework which we are able to build out of our environment?

The individual within the family

When the child is born, it emerges from the physical womb into the outer world only to be contained for many years to come within the family relationship. Just as the embryo was fed by the mother's blood until it was sufficiently mature to leave the protection of her body, so the personality of the child is nourished during the early years in healthy circumstances by a subtle interrelationship with his parents, father as well as mother, sisters and brothers, or whoever serves or extends the parental role. Within this human framework the forces of the body and of the psyche are free to expand in accordance with their own nature, so that the child can grow and play and work his way towards maturity.

For the development of a healthy child, the essential ingredient is inner and outer security—he needs to feel safe in his daily world and also in the undoubtedness of his budding little person. He should be able to take this for granted like the air he breathes. Unpossessive love and understanding nourish his emotional life and give him the sense of belongingness essential to satisfactory personal growth and adequate adaptation to the world of outer reality. Throughout his life his happiness and sense of well-being and his ability to stand stresses and strains may depend largely on this early experience of security and freedom to be himself, within the boundary walls of family discipline.

If, however, as a child he has to be constantly on guard to protect the right of his individuality—for instance, against becoming the little husband to the mother or to maintain the security of the home by being the father to his younger brothers and sisters—then his development will be disturbed, distorted and handicapped at least to some extent. Certain aspects of living will be prematurely experienced and others, for instance the need to play, will be arrested and perhaps never expressed, so that they remain an aching void and possibly a source of later neurosis. Parts of the personality get 'entombed'. From this 'tomb' come radiations, vague and indefinite, but very potent and disturbing to the conscious personality.

As the child grows older, his original dependence progressively lessens and changes through a succession of human bridges, relationships such as to aunts, uncles, the milkman, the old gardener, teachers, schoolmates and friends; at an important stage such as puberty he may still need his parents but in a different way from his earlier years.

Ideally, when the time comes to step over the threshold of the family circle into the world, problems no longer need to be referred to father or mother, but to those appropriate centres in his own personality which have been developed through the years of these interrelationships.

The process of development from birth to maturity means the gradual taking over into one's self of the authority previously invested in the parental world.

The ancestral background

We have been looking at the individual in his expansion outwardly over the surface of his young world. We will now ask: how has he come to be there, at this place and the present time? He stands at the apex of a pyramid or cone, the base of which is set deep in the past. Below him are his parents, his grandparents and

earlier ancestors, the people of his nation, his race, mankind as a
whole; and at the remote beginnings of his being, some five
hundred million years away, is animal and plant life and the
original sources from which all life springs. With all this he is in
direct physical continuity. It may shake us to feel this as a fact.

The individual is thus linked up with his historical background,
to which he for ever belongs, with his ancestral tail as Jung has
called it, from which he can never be separated as long as he lives.
But if he turns only to his ancestral stream for sustenance, he is
bound to perish. One needs also a forward-going towardness, a
sense of destiny, a sense of God (however he may be experienced),
to hold and guide us onward, so that life is held or swings between
two poles—the past with the continuity of time out of which we
come and the future with a sense of destination which calls us and
towards which we go.

Not infrequently, a neurosis is conditioned by the attempt the
individual has made to amputate himself from this tail, as for
instance the man who tries to live as if he were entirely mind or
entirely spirit or entirely body or, say, the son of a butcher who
repudiates his humble origin because he thinks it would stand in
the way of his career. When a man does this, it is as though he were
trying to live the life of someone not himself.

It is only by discovering, and coming to terms with, the values
of his own ancestral heritage that he can be freed of its apparent
burden or downward pull, and so be ready to experience
consciously its positive forward-going quality.

Man's inheritance is a storehouse of undiscovered potentialities.
One could say that the roots of the psyche reach down into the
remote past like the roots of a tree, drawing life-giving moisture
and nourishment from the soil in which they grow. This 'soil',
which we now call the collective unconscious, is the seed-bed out
of which man has to be formed and try to mould himself and his
life in the world according to his unique pattern and from the sum
total of psychic energy with which he is born. It is a part of his life's
task to grow aware of his capacity, to become conscious and thus
to co-operate actively with his growing individuality. In other
words, he has to nurture and encourage his developing consciousness so as to co-operate with, give personalness to, his life movement. *Out of—along—towards:* to link up that which is behind and
within him, his inner 'personalness' and value, with his ego, that
strange, two-edged gift of the gods, so that he can be freed from
the feeling of burden, into a sense of forward activity, of becoming-
ness. This may well lead him to the discovery of, and link up with,

that which is greater than us, and seen, as it were, in *front* of us. We say *Life calls*, *God calls*, and we need to hear and try to answer it.

From his first tentative explorations into the world of external reality, the child, if all goes well, proceeds naturally through the successive stages of his personality development. As the ego develops, he draws further and further away from his former state of identity with the collective unconscious and normally takes as his own the commonly accepted ideals of his social group, the conscious values of his environment. His identification with each successive widening circle of his environment in turn is a part of his growth till, finally, he can achieve personal stability. His goal at maturity is to fulfil his individual, as well as his collective, obligations.

Latent starting points of neurosis

This, however, is a task that requires single-minded effort and concentration of energy, and it is to be expected that certain values of life which interfere with its realisation will be pushed aside, be repressed or remain undeveloped. These neglected qualities may be vital aspects of the personality which are of such significance to the individual that he cannot live satisfactorily without them; they may be important units of the mosaic of the psyche, highly charged with specialised energy. When such factors are forced or allowed to drop out of conscious life, they are transferred to the dark sphere of the psyche, the unconscious, carrying their charge of energy with them. And since this energy is now excluded from active life and without channels for its expression, it continues to work underground.

On the other hand, the ego is robbed of exactly that amount, so that the conscious directed life of the individual has less than the quantum of energy that is needed for satisfactory living. If this is not adjusted and there is already too much energy attached to unrealised potentialities lying in the unconscious, these factors assume control or, at least, interfere effectively with spontaneous progression: the individual may get caught, bogged down. If continued for too long, this loss of balance is profoundly disturbing. He feels threatened in his very being, becomes anxious and fearful (often masquerading as aggression), and he or she may even develop hysterical or obsessional symptoms. Their life comes more or less to a standstill, caught in the vicious circle of what might be called an unrecognised neurosis.

In particular, at every transitional stage of life — weaning, commencement of school, adolescence, leaving home, marriage, the approach of middle age, of old age — there is a tendency to linger in the past, to cling to the kind of adaptation which till then has proven tolerably satisfactory and in which one feels at home. Perhaps one of the most critical phases in the individual's growth is the separation of his psychic energy from its dependence on the parents.

If, for instance, the child has been deprived by fate from having the full experience of the personal mother relationship, he may in severe cases remain attached to the powerful mother figure in his ancestral background which Jung has described as the mother archetype. Then, in crucial situations which demand his energy to go forward, he cannot free himself from this attachment and actually shrinks back like a child towards his mother. He may even go through life for ever seeking her, desperately hoping to find his personal significance, to be de-orphaned and become redeemed. A child that has been orphaned, actually or psychologically, tends to remain tied to his incompleteness. He has a wound that ever calls him back, we can say, so that he may attend to its healing, on the way to greater wholeness.

In later life, this attitude might well be regarded as regressive, as an escape from outer responsibilities. But recognised in its inner significance, it is a necessity, an attempt to save his threatened life. If, however, by the power of will he would try to counteract this backward pull, he would either become more and more rigid and dogmatic and personally depleted, or else compromise, make do and get along reasonably well. On the other hand, if his sense of values was strong enough, he would rather perish than forsake his inner loyalty. It may need a breakdown to discover the significance of his so-called regression and, with appropriate help, to go back to the area of the original deprivation and slowly and gradually build up a new way into life.

The collapse of the old attitude

As I said before and Jung repeatedly emphasises, a neurosis is far from being a purely negative happening. Looked at from one point of view, it is an effort on the part of the psyche to force into consciousness certain essential values which have been denied life. One might even call it an attempt of the unconscious to compel the individual to search for new ways. Neurosis can reveal the extent of distortion from his natural psychological pattern or structure; if he takes on his illness, it can become a great opportunity, as it draws his attention to the unrealised richness of the totality of his being. It gives him an incentive, indeed turns into a necessity, to attend to the understanding and modification of his distortion and to strive towards developing a way of life more in harmony with his instinctive nature.

This tendency of the unconscious to correct an adaptation that was on too restricted a base was vividly exemplified to me by a woman patient of twenty-six years who was admitted to an observation ward during my work there (see page 47). She was an intelligent and lively personality who, after ten years of mechanical work in a factory, had a breakdown—the escape from too narrow a life into phantasy had finally led to a state of acute dissociation. She had to stay for several months in a mental hospital. After her discharge she came back to me for a long course of psychotherapy, during which it became possible to develop her dormant gifts and capabilities. Eventually she could build up satisfying personal relationships and become a child care officer. I learned more and more that neurosis has to be approached with the attitude demanded by its creative potential. We have to treat the tentative budding of the new possibilities which emerge from the unconscious with the tender care that all new-born creatures require. Otherwise two things will happen: (1) the patient will suffer from an unjustifiable feeling of inferiority; and (2) the positive energy contained in the experience will not be released. One could say that the neurosis is the patient's problem child. Both patient and therapist have to employ the same kind of wisdom in dealing with it that wise parents need in helping a child to grow through and beyond its problem. As we have just seen, it may take a severe breakdown, even a psychosis, to prepare the way for the discovery and expression of the individual's real values. The word 'breakdown', which is generally used in a depreciatory sense and even in an abusive way, can just as appropriately be used positively, since in relation to neurosis it means the collapse of an adaptation which is *inappropriate* for the individual—it may have been outgrown or become too narrow and restricted, or even be one which never did really belong to that person's pattern of life.

In neurosis, the individual has allowed himself, or had been forced by inner or outer circumstances, to deviate too far from his natural pattern, so that a portion of it has become split off and is working in opposition to the total psyche. One could say that the ego is like the chairman of a board of directors and that the various aspects of the personality are its members. Each one contributes his particular part, and together they form a working team. In the neurotic situation, it is as though one or more members of the board are secretly acting contrary to the policy of the whole. In such a split or dissociation, one might find the anti-life element. In his book, *Mythology of the Soul*, Baynes* aptly calls this rebel or deserter element the renegade factor.

It is important to realise that in the original situation the renegade may have been right in his rebellion, as for instance in the case of a man of about forty. He dreamed that he was watching a lively young boy of eight or nine attempting to push open the door of a walled garden in which he rightfully belonged. Within the garden, standing against the door, was a dour, lazy, supercilious bully of about twenty. The sturdy young boy pushed with his hands and threw himself against the door in his effort to get it open. But the bully easily kept the door shut. Finally, the little fellow put his back against the door, dug in his heels and, in an agony of effort, as though his very existence depended on it, as indeed it did, he succeeded in forcing open the door into the garden which was his. The patient's parents had died when he was five and he had spent the rest of his childhood in surroundings antipathetic to the free and happy atmosphere of his earlier days. He instinctively knew that his real individuality was not accepted. This felt like a violation. Although he was unable to stand up consciously to the weight of his unfriendly environment, he refused within himself to submit. This refusal was healthy, but it also produced a poisoned attitude towards authority. Thus a reversal came about in which the boy in the dream, symbolising his original nature, was pushed out of the garden and the youth, representing a reluctant compromise with the world, got inside. The dream is trying to correct this false situation, and it needs all the passion of the boy's instinctive inherited truth to break through that door.

In fact, the dreamer had to meet the bully as an inner aspect of himself quite seriously on his own ground, and in what Jung has called active imagination, talk with him and listen to what he had to say. Gradually the part of the personality which he represented lost its renegade character and was brought back into co-operation with the rest of his psyche. When the patient can experience such negative aspects and accept them as part of himself, their autonomous character can change, so that they come more or less in relationship to, and under the control of, the ego.

Such meaningful phantasies, much as the creation of symbols, are a natural function of the psyche. In childhood, they form the

*H. G. Baynes, *Mythology of the Soul* (Baillière, Tindall & Cox, London 1940), pp. 3, 40, 89, 96, 264, 552, 629, 774.

bridge that leads the child over from identity with the unconscious and with his surroundings into consciousness. Symbols are like guiding stars which beckon him onward from stage to stage of life. The anticipatory experiencing of a phantasy or relationship to a symbol brings about the appropriate attitude for his adaptation to new situations. We could say that the vision leads to the attitude and the attitude to adaptation, so that step by step the child goes forward towards maturity.

It is by the same creative process that a patient finds his way out of a neurosis back into life. The symbols emerging from the unconscious in dreams and phantasies can reveal their meaning through the collaboration of patient and analyst, and the patient learns how to integrate the knowledge he gains about himself into everyday living.

It often happens that the individual's most significant positive values are born into life only after he has experienced highly charged negative aspects of the unconscious. If, during analysis, he can accept these, the negative factor is, in some mysterious way, freed from its most disturbing and disagreeable aspects, and there follows a feeling of healing, of becoming a more integrated being. This means also that he now has to carry his own cross — he can no longer project these parts of his shadow on to others.

Differentiation

Another task of analysis with regard to the unconscious consists in differentiating between what belongs to the individual psyche and what to collective experience. Many people go through life bowed down with a burden of guilt which is not personally theirs, or carrying the problem of a member of their family. I remember a professional man, just under forty years of age, who came to me because of attacks of writer's cramp which occurred at times of special stress. These did not interfere with his work as a whole, in which he was efficient and successful. He was happily married, with two young children, and enjoyed his work. Except for the symptom of writer's cramp there was little to indicate any problem. Analysis, however, revealed that actually all his life he had been living under a serious interference with the full expression of his individual nature. He had a brother, ten years older than himself, who from the patient's earliest years had constantly tried to inhibit his spontaneous expression, and this continued up to early manhood. A considerable portion of his personality was under the shadow of this influence which created tensions and anxiety (usually successfully concealed). One felt

that only his exceptionally sound personality had prevented the
problem from coming up long before. He was very gifted, with
considerable musical talent, while his brother was a rather tight
and inhibited man; ironically, he was called 'father' by the members of his staff, not because of a helpful fatherly attitude but
because he was constantly engaged in admonishing someone.
This 'family pattern' had already begun to repeat itself in the
next generation. One day when my patient was correcting his
son, aged four, 'who', he said, 'is just like I was', his wife remarked:
'You sound like your brother Charles.' When during our work
he first began to 'doodle', he made the most meticulous drawings
—the lines must be absolutely straight, strictly parallel, etc. But
after a time he produced a spontaneous coloured picture of
something like an abscess which had been full of pus and was
now open and draining, commenting: 'I just had to let myself go.'

Only after this patient had won insight into the deeper causes
of Charles's tightness did he become able to separate his individual psyche from that of his brother, regain the energy that had
been attached to the elder brother archetype, and use it in everyday life. We should be aware that we are not personally responsible
for having been born into a particular family or generation with
its peculiar problems, but it sometimes takes a neurosis to make
us discover this and get free from it.

The second half of life

We will now consider some aspects of neurosis as it may occur
specially in the second half of life.

Jung beautifully compares man's life with the journey of the
sun across the sky. It rises from the darkness out of the sea in the
east and during the morning climbs higher and higher, sending
out its rays over a wider and wider horizon, until it reaches its
full powers at midday in the zenith. Then, as the forward movement continues, it descends, withdrawing its rays by slow degrees
until it finally passes down into the darkness again.

The child and the youth have to differentiate themselves from
the unconscious by turning away from it to the outer world. In
the puberty of the teens, the hold of the family should give way
to the development of the ego. In the first half of life, the psychic
energy can be expressed satisfactorily through the process of
establishing oneself as an effective contributing member of one's
social group. Life's values then lie more in the external world. If,
however, these basic phases of development cannot be achieved
and the adolescent gets, so to speak, stuck in a pattern that he

should have outgrown, the arrested life stream may produce disturbances which might call for psychotherapeutic help, thus preventing a later severe neurosis.

The beginning of middle age is a kind of second puberty which takes place on a higher turn of the spiral of life, and the process is in a way the reverse of the earlier puberty. The predominance of the ego now needs to yield to the demands of the totality of one's being, the self. This does not mean that man should repudiate his social achievements or withdraw from life. What it does mean is a new emphasis, a new priority of values, a fresh relationship to earlier aims and potentials that had hitherto remained in the shadow world. At middle age, the psychic energy begins to activate the unlived life, those aspects of the personality that have not been, or could not be, developed during the process of external adaptation. The psychic pattern is not complete until this westward-flowing energy is also recognised in its significance: the mature man, as far as he is humanly able, has to come to terms with these realities within himself. The meaning of life and its inner values remain to be discovered. In old age, near the end, his energy may well withdraw more and more into himself until finally, when the physical body passes out of life, he is self-contained in his own psyche.

The businessman

One patient in particular enabled me to gain a clear picture of the typical problem of neurosis in the second half of life. He was a successful businessman of middle age, recently retired. As a boy and youth he lived an active, many-sided and colourful life. Then he was caught up by the idea of making his way in the world, of founding a business and becoming wealthy. Most of his former activities were abandoned because they stood in the way of his concentrated ambition. He did not marry and left his church because such relationships would divert his attention from his goal. His life became narrow and materialistic, but in a few years he built up a business which brought him money and prestige.

He reached middle age, married and was about to retire and enjoy his well-earned leisure when he discovered to his horror that three things were happening to him: (1) his everyday life which had been always full of zest had become flat and uninteresting; (2) vague, unexplainable fears and apprehensions were assailing him, and (3) a variety of physical symptoms were disturbing his peace of mind. These symptoms and fears came to fill more and more of his conscious life till it was almost taken possession of by these irrational manifestations from the unconscious. It was as if the neglected part of his life had sent out an SOS to make him take steps to correct the balance. All the unlived, rejected aspects of his personality, so to speak, waiting in the unconscious, had become charged with energy and were clamouring for recognition. The irrational manifestations appeared negative and destructive because they had formerly been repudiated.

Taking the conscious and the unconscious parts of the personality as a pair of opposites, when one of them is overcharged with energy, one part is overweighted, overspecialised, overvalued, their equilibrium is upset and life is felt to be threatened. Anxiety makes its appearance, and it is significant that an irrational fear of death was actually one of this man's chief complaints. As is so often the case, he felt his grasp slipping from his present way of life yet clung rigidly to it. The more he sensed the urgency of the irrational, the more rational he became, the more he bolstered up his old attitude. We can readily sympathise with him in his dilemma—understandably he held fast to the aims which had brought him success, security and prestige. But this very rigidity, this refusal to admit the opposite, the unlived side, was a sure sign of doubt about the absoluteness of the truth he so vehemently defended.

During his analysis he had to learn that the dawn of this new stage of life called for reorientation—that which had been given the greatest value needed to make a place beside it for other values clamouring for recognition. Indeed, in order to regain his health, he had no choice. Just as the first half of his life had been directed towards the attainment of outer goals, so now he had to be willing to turn his attention inward. For by consciously relating to the unknown realm of the unconscious, he would encounter not only his personal shadow side but discover a whole new world, the world of the archetypes, to enliven him, renew him and widen and deepen his life. Hence, with the mature person, the emphasis will be on adaptation to the *inner* reality, whereas in treating the neurosis of youth, the symbolic material produced from the unconscious is, generally speaking, considered more in terms of adaptation to the *outer* world. The task is to bring into consciousness, and integrate, unconscious aspects and tendencies, so that one is able to live a more complete life in accordance with one's own natural psychic structure. Jung calls this development the process of individuation.

To heal means to make whole. The healing factors which restore health are indeed those which in the beginning produced the illness, the neurosis.

As unconscious contents are made conscious and assimilated, both the shadow and the ego are modified. The ego adaptation loses some of its onesidedness in allowing expression to aspects of the shadow, and by being accepted and integrated, the shadow is separated from its identity with the collective unconscious. In a very subtle way the conscious and the unconscious aspects of the personality are brought together into an entity, into a new centre of *individuality* which is neither ego nor the unconscious but includes both.

Helped by one's guide (and who can say what cloak of office he may wear?), one may be able to go down into the frightening chaos, and with his aid learn to understand and accept its dark and hidden message. Thus, within the limits which our life allows us, can we follow the vision of completeness, the experiencing of life as whole, with all its varying aspects of light and shadow. It is a royal task under the authority of that centre which Jung has called the self, and beyond that, we might say, of God.

ON THE STRUGGLE OF THE EGO BETWEEN THE INNER AND THE OUTER WORLD (1957)

It is a vital problem to recognise the central role the ego plays in the struggle between the inner and the outer world, as revealed and developed in analysis. Most of us, during its earlier phases as well as in the early stages of childhood and youth, need to be helped to grow out of the young, and basically necessary, phase of *egocentricity* and so recognise the 'you', and beyond the 'you' the self, the totality which the ego is meant to serve. In reviewing the practice of analytical psychology, I feel that one-sided emphasis is laid too early on what is called the self. It appears not only appropriate but essential once more to reaffirm the significance of the ego. It needs to feel and to be established in experience before it can really be related to the self. Otherwise, I have found, the ensuing ego – self relationship is a more or less wilful, intellectual one, to a large extent an artefact or even an ego-prestige construct.

Deep analysis, when it goes well, becomes directed from some central part of the psyche which one supposes is either the self or in relationship to it, a kind of nucleus of authority in our total personality. This can be felt and becomes more obvious when some figures in a dream often recur, though not always in the same guise or form, and act as the guide of the soul, as *psycho-pompos*. In one series of a patient's dreams this figure repeatedly came up as 'the conductor'.

Function of the ego in the total personality

The ego is the carrier of consciousness, a differentiator or a co-ordinator, and within its realm has an integrating function. The ego is like an organ of the total personality which, as manifested in a human individual, naturally includes body, mind and soul. Although, say, a heart can be examined in itself, it cannot really exist in isolation and has to be assessed in relationship to other organs, the total body, and this is similar with the ego.

How does *ideally a healthy ego work*? Like the prime minister of a state or the executive of a big firm or factory, the firm being the total psyche in relation to the inner and outer world; perhaps still more aptly, it might be compared with the head or parental authority in charge of a large family. This inner family, if I may call it so, corresponds to those aspects or complexes of the psyche which specially manifest themselves as individuals in dreams, phantasies, etc. — those parts which are near enough to consciousness and have enough continuity to be related to and personified. To continue the comparison, it might be a family of the old-fashioned size, mixed of boys and girls of different ages up to young adulthood; they represent different facets of the psyche, all of which contribute a certain individual value and standpoint, each of them of body as well as spirit. The parental task is protection against the outer world and mediating its demands, and likewise to look after and co-ordinate the needs of the children from within. In picturing this family, I must add (and it was really quite an omission) that animals too belong to it, the dogs and the cats, the horse and, maybe, the birds. All these and many other pets and treasures belong and add to the domain in which the ego is the devoted, caring and, very often, burdened authority. I apply the word ego to the one that turns up as I, whom I feel is me, as the conscious executive of the individual psyche. He is the one who is finally responsible for the translation of the psyche's dreams, phantasies, hunches into moment-to-moment, hour-to-hour and day-to-day activities in the actual environment.

To repeat, the ego is the executive of these inner aspects of the psyche in the here and now. The well-being in relationship to the outer and the inner world depends on its loving, understanding and continuous care. From all this one may gather what it means and demands of the ego so that it can do its work effectively and hold its position healthily, with zest and joy.

The hero ego

I am continually impressed in my clinical work by the heroic effort and struggle of this little portion of individual consciousness called ego. Not just vegetating or living behind barriers, not just keeping afloat, but growing and reaching out for meaning and expression, it has to maintain itself in a life-supporting way, with the powers of the collective unconscious behind it and the expectations of the collective social life, such as having to earn a living, in front of and around it.

It is the devotion and hard work of the ego, the facing of terrors and the acceptance of joy, the carrying of tension and of burdens, the standing up for one's innermost values, which so impress me that in analytical work I sometimes feel I am associating with a hero and with heroes. And, indeed, it is the ego as the carrier of consciousness that makes the life of the psyche humanly possible.

There is no archetype, individually speaking, without this little hero ego. The archetypes are there, I am sure, but it is only when part of them becomes illuminated by some reflection of light, of consciousness, from the ego that an individual can talk of an archetype in relation to himself, that really Jungian psychology comes into being, not merely Jungian terminology.

In this respect, analysis can sometimes call to mind the tales of the hero in antiquity, fairy tales and folklore, who had to undertake a great journey and meet many hazards, face many dangers, each of which challenged, tempted, tried him to the uttermost, each of which he had to pass through in order to be ready for the next phase, until finally he finds the treasure or the human being or the companion which he needs to reach the fullness of his stature, of himself. And so, equipped with more developed potentials, he can live more fully rather than unduly partially. *The hero in this sense is the one who brings his individuality into life,* who differentiates from the mass and who carries the burden and the gleam of his uniqueness, his divine spark, into the realm of human expression, thus fulfilling his life and destiny.

To add a word on the hero's path: I take to be essentially and ultimately friendly forces the witches, devils and dragons that guard the treasure, assail or challenge him at boundaries or transitional places. They are really the searching examiners of the readiness, the state of maturity of the hero. If he does not pass them, if he cannot meet their challenges, then it would be unsafe to insist and he would risk destruction even if by hard will he could pass on to the next phase. So we take them as in fact being on the hero's side, and not against him as they can so readily appear to be.

We will now look at different phases in the development of the ego, pointing out some of the vital stations in its growth and formation up to young manhood and womanhood. The emphasis will be on such critical moments and influences when the ego is specially prone to injury and on such values, essential to its health, which, if damaged too deeply or for too long, bring about disturbances and illness of the personality, including those manifesting themselves in later life.

Phases of the growth and development

There are significant stations in the growth and formation of the ego which all of us have to go through, from the time when we may still relatively warmly and safely be contained in a secure home in the early phase, say up to two and three years, and from there grow forth in a succession of critical buddings, each coming out of the previously established phase, till finally we reach adultness. When all goes well, we attain a rightfully self-confident sense of ourselves and an equally secure sense of relationship to the outside world.

I call the early phase of mother containment, up to two to three years, the golden egg stage. Within it, there can be a good deal of damage already at birth, as well as during feeding and weaning time, or if at an early age the baby had to be rushed off to hospital for a sudden illness, etc. If the shock has not been too severe, the individual may later on receive much help from analytical treatment.

We will leave out in this context the struggles a baby may experience during interuterine life and in the breast stage because we are here concerned mainly with damage which the adult has been able to remember or recover the memory of, which can be brought into consciousness during analysis. I want to discuss such critical stages predominantly from the psychology of the adult rather than from the point of view of child psychology.

Let us take what I think is one of the *basic principles in establishing the ego*. Each new activity, as it buds out from a potential to an actuality, needs first to be experienced *freely* and *spontaneously* without expectations or responsibilities and not felt to be imposed even by friendly and meaningful authority. As an example, the child, boy or girl, passes from the free, uninterfered with, natural phase of expression to that when he is expected to be trained to be, and one hopes learning to enjoy being, 'clean and dry'. If, however, he is coerced into it, say, at twelve months, in rivalry to the little girl next door who attains that condition easily at this age, whereas this one's natural time is, say, eighteen months, then here and now is developed in the ego a sense of being under, of having to live up to, *expectations* which are significantly out of step with his instinctual rhythm.

The question of expectation is rather a tricky problem. It is wrong in the manner just described, but even when the expectations are right for the child and its age, they may still have a harmful effect if not given in a loving way but divorced from the relationship with the child, say, out of the mother's own needs or the nurse's principles. The child feels this only too well.

Ego establishment

The golden egg time which has its own great joys as well as hazards is followed by the establishment of the individual as an I, as himself, the phase to which we have to come back quite often in our analytical work. This stage is usually most marked between three and six years and is extended in a maturing way, onwards up to the teenage, up to early manhood or early womanhood; each spiral has its stage of self-assertion. This phase, as you know, is one that is given great attention, and not only in the studies of childhood. Ideally, a tremendous effort is made by the group and the family to establish the child's I-ness or security in its identity. This traditional emphasis shows how important it is and was always instinctively felt to be, and the amount of detailed and continuous attention that is required. That, of course, is the ideal way. Then the child becomes identified with its name and resents strongly being called by, or mistaken for, another: 'I am not my sister — I am I'; when it becomes jealous of its toys and possessions or of their being used as general property. It is then when birthdays become a special and important occasion.

Many of us have had a lack at this time of growth and establishment in one form or another. Although we are able to overcome such damage to some extent, the question is whether this can be done significantly. Most likely, almost inevitably, it will leave a special sensitivity, a touchiness at those places. Here is a very vital point I would like to draw attention to. I believe that *a child is born with a sense of its dignity, of its royalty*. To see the little girl in the pram, the little boy in this golden age stage with his undoubtedness, to see them move and dance to music, gives you the feeling there is the little princess and there is a royal child. In some, a very few, this is maintained throughout this critical period, defended at all costs, and their natural dignity may carry them right through life.

But in others, their self-assertion and the establishment of their individuality come up against harassed parents, themselves in difficult circumstances, and so these young children are what is called 'broken in' — or, can we say, broken up in some cases. Their natural dignity is damaged, and this is a serious damage which is noticeable when they have to carry their own flag into a world which, although not hostile, anyway does not look upon undue individuality with much friendliness. This characteristic is true down to the animal world. As a trainer of animals knows, you must be very careful not to damage their sense of dignity. This is true of dogs, of horses and, I am sure, of many other animals. (We all know or have heard of the horsebreaker whom you never send your young pony to and the other one whom you are only too glad to.)

When the child comes out of the original golden undoubted-ness into an awareness through which one obtains differentiation, the sense of right and wrong is aroused, of pleasing and dis-pleasing others, belonging to and not belonging to, and of greater objectivity. From the moment *the consciousness of one's own identity is born*, self-consciousness may also come in, even doubt and insecurity. Then a special form of caring love is needed for healthy growth, or at least a certain minimum of support and guidance, appropriate to the individual. But how many have had it? It is here that analysis may bring hope where previously there had been despair.

The need for education

Once the child has grown up enough and needs to be educated, licked into shape as we say of the animal world, fitted into the social pattern of family and tribe, there may come a critical time both for the child and the parents. It is not that every detail needs to be right and exact and the child must not be at all hurt or over-run. But ideally, though not often met with in analysis, the child needs to feel all along that it is within a loving circle, accepted and not rejected as him or herself even when told off or punished. If this caring attitude is maintained, then a great deal of mistaken handling can take place without serious damage. But however right the detail may be by the textbook, if this framework is not sound, not warmly appropriate for that child individually, then all the detailed socialisation will be of no avail to enable him or her to go intact and secure enough into the outer world: 'Mother did everything correct except that I never felt she really loved me,' as one of my students put it.

It is most necessary for the child to feel that there are boundaries to the garden, that there are limits to behaviour or self-assertion within a situation, that there is some definite No at critical occasions in its environment. But what should not happen is that he feels a No as a total rejection and prohibition of himself as himself. Otherwise, there may be an abandonment of himself, in which case his individuality is left behind or he becomes a rebel, isolated instead of healthily differentiated. This sense of a need of a boundary and guidance can be very strong in an intelligent child. As one of about seven years who had been for a year or two at a very free and easy school, when mother rather apprehensively told him that he was going to another school, exclaimed: 'Oh, Mother, I do hope it is a school where you have to learn. I don't want any more of this whiffy-whaffy sort of school.'

Living under expectations

Here I would like to say that one of the most critical situations arises when the child is too inappropriately handled for too long so that, in order to get that minimum sense of loving belongingness which every child needs, as a plant requires a minimum of water and sunshine, he may give up in despair living out of his own centre and will act according to the expectations of others. This will bring him the approval and feeling of belonging which are so essential to survival. However, if this false adaptation becomes chronic, as unfortunately it too often does, then the child is established in a counterfeit style of living — counterfeit to his individuality. He will fear to act from his own centre and will always ask or look for what others may expect of him: Will they agree with me? Will they approve of me? Thus, when a child is forced to leave his own centre for need of affection and acts according to expectation, he may well lose his self-assertion and initiative — in other words, the straightforward growth of his young personality is interfered with. This situation may arise in what is really a sound and good family, innocently for instance when the mother's interest may flow more to another brother or sister. Even with the greatest care, when the new baby comes along, the older one may have, say, the measles or a whooping cough, and mother being unable to look after him as usual, his undoubtedness may be shaken.

Incidentally, we should never forget that parents have their own troubles and difficulties, their own unhappiness, and one can easily fall into the very gross error of depreciating and blaming the parents because their son or daughter has failed to achieve what one feels he or she potentially could. In the child who feels he has to live up to expectations, the counterpole to his outward passivity and obedience, i.e. the aggression that arises from this violation of himself, is buried deeply. It contains so much vigour that the energy system of the child is damaged, and only after long and deep therapy that aggressiveness, of bomb-like explosive power, often of murderous intensity, may come out.

Rebel children

In another type of situation, the opposition will come out at once and the child will become the rebel. Then he takes a stand for his own individuality and for the sense of his values, however inappropriately this may turn out owing to his inexperience. This courageous young rebel with his integrity may be enabled to take his flag into the world, if in time he can find some older experienced person to see behind the antisocial behaviour the value this young individual is carrying, so that he feels appreciated and can come out of his isolation. Otherwise there is the danger that he will go into blind rebellious behaviour and may degenerate into what we might call a delinquent.

On the other hand, there is another type of rebel, the child who has given up all hope of being understood by the family or significant members of it and, without visibly opposing society, turns to his own inner world and starts to live from there. This may happen if, at the early age of four or five years onwards, the child is unable to establish a satisfactory relationship to his environment. His psychic energy then turning inwards, he may find a significant place which enables him to hold his identity as himself, a treasure house within. This can become a source of inspiration throughout his life, from which he makes his own individual mark in the world in the uniqueness of his expression, be it as an artist, a story-teller, an inventor, a specialist in a particular field. Yet, however great the achievement, there remains a critical area of isolation. So let us realise what price has to be paid for it.

Substitute parents

We must never forget that a child needs parents. That is an instinctive, an archetypal need, and if he cannot find it satisfied in the ordinary natural place, then with his own instinct, intelligence and limited experience, he will seek it out elsewhere, in a substitute parent he may pick up anywhere outside, be it on the farm, in the stable yard, in a shop, or in the gang, in a football team, and so on.

It need not be among humans where the parental friend is found, it may be a world of one's own discovery that brings salvation from fatal isolation. We know from the poets, Hölderlin for instance, that he grew up with the trees. It is related of the great Lord Haldane that as a small boy he used to have moods which came over him and he would go into a beech wood and there embrace, put his arms round, a large beech tree, stay there for five to fifteen minutes and then go back home and feel once more contained within himself, consoled and strengthened.

So far, we have three groups that emerge from the struggle of the ego with the inner and the outer world. The first, out of a desperate need for survival, the urgent necessity to be accepted and loved, gives up the hope of acting out of his individuality and begins his span of life by acting out of the *expectations of others*, hoping that by playing up to them he will be accepted and belong. For no one can live and survive healthily in complete isolation. This is the paradox of the individual. He needs to be alone as an individual, but in order to live he also has to relate to others. These are two pulls from which one of the main tensions of our lives is created: the need to be alone and that to relate and belong are both fundamental.

The second group is that of the *rebel* who, in order to save his individuality and his values, has to fight first his immediate surroundings and then, maybe, the world.

The third group gives up hope of being accepted or understood by his immediate environment but, out of the richness and imagery of his own nature, finds a place beyond and below these surroundings. It may, as we said, be in substitute parents, in animals or in trees, in some concept or sense of values that seems to come out of his own nature, to stem almost directly from the archetypal world, in a way that may even bring a sense of having a direct relationship with God. Here is a danger, though, of losing the earth and becoming a fanatic.

The orphaned

There is, however, another group, and quite a widespread one, which I call the orphaned—the bloodsuckers, the vampires. Their empty ego, despairing of its self-valuation, gets possessed by its own hunger and so goes around, as it were, to swallow the world into itself, to appropriate other people's attention, in extreme cases even stealing their gloves, copying their dress, etc. Unless this is modified, it can go on to an almost manic state because these acquisitions do not feed or enrich the grasping ego, and so it may become insatiable in the way of trying to fill up its hungry emptiness. Such an ego cannot and does not truly recognise, nor relate to, any 'you'. No gift, however great, seems to be able to activate its own resources from which it might rightfully be fed; warm gratitude seems impossible. It is as if such beings require constant transfusions of other people's blood, but because their own bloodmaking resources remain inactive, far from getting their health restored, they get more and more isolated and humanly desiccated.

The basic importance of the I–Thou relationship becomes evident here. It is a development of maturity; the Thou is recognised as a human being in its own right and with its own needs. As long as it is predominantly projected, there is no real relationship at all—it remains a mirror effect and will finally lead to frustration.

Sudden reversals

Though, for the purposes of study, we distinguish these groups, actually they are hardly ever found in pure form. There will always be people who, out of the upsurge of the opposite from their depth, might suddenly do something which their environment would say was impossible for them to do, the last thing they expected of them. We think, for instance, of those who have rejected all ordered authority, have, say, gone into the communist movement or deliberately broken all the traditional taboos, have rejected father and mother and then, apparently suddenly, though probably slowly incubating this in their depth, embrace the father/mother Church and go, say, into Roman Catholicism.

Others who had been living meticulously by the expectations of their environment and keeping the traditional line immaculately, will unexpectedly go over into the opposite and assert themselves. Jung quotes* the example of a man who had been a most conventional father of the family, a teacher in the Sunday school and church warden, who sat up in bed one early morning and exclaimed to his astonished wife: 'I have been a damned hypocrite all my life and I am done with the whole damned lot,' and from then on, to the dismay of his family, instead of carefully guarding the family fortunes, etc., spent them as he felt like doing and, I dare say, he

*Probably C. G. Jung, *Collected Works*, Vol. 8 (2nd edn. London 1969), par. 775 is referred to.

seemed on the whole a healthier man for it or, anyway more human.

School

After these digressions we come to a further step in the young child's development into the world, a new stage in ego maturing. He now starts growing out of the family where he has been exploring, discovering and responding to the everyday knocks a child gets and to the everyday wonders a child finds. He is now going to step out of the family home and garden into the stream of life outside the family, into his first school. How he establishes himself there is of vital significance to his well-being, to the subsequent sense of his own values and the relationship of his I to the Thou of others.

It is most important how he lives, feels and moves and has his being in this new adventure, how he takes root in this phase of the outside world, how he finds his bearings in the stream of life of his generation and of his own time. Meeting his contemporaries, his own age group, outside the known and accustomed family situation, if he is fortunate he will find new wonders and new discoveries. He will discover not only the quickening of the heart in making friends of his own, he will also meet the wonders of thinking, of words, phrases, writing, of numbers, etc., the sense of being set free, of reading on his own when he wants to, not just pretending to read or hearing others recite to him when it suits them. With the use of his intelligence, with the growth of his intellect and experience he becomes freer from the parental needs and expectations, from the family situation; he takes up a new and more independent place in the family.

If all goes well, there will be a more or less smooth transition from the world of day-dreams into that of reality which brings a quality of wonder different from anything the child found in his plays and fairy tales. Now, through reading and learning, he can relate to people even in other countries, to other ways of life, other times. Here he feels the beginnings of belonging to the world, which widens his basis and decreases his dependence—all-important only a short time ago—on the family and on whether he is 'good' or 'bad' within the home. I want to emphasise the significance of this zestful discovering of the outer world, of the child's establishing itself in it and of getting the joyful feeling of his own reach and powers, of being an adventurer in life. Because when this, or an appreciable amount of it, is missed, then a healthy ego development is held up at least in part, suspended, and decades later we may find during analysis that patients have to recover this stage.

It is during these school years that, on a new round of the spiral and perhaps with a pal of his very own, the child becomes aware of himself, of his potentialities, of the skills which he can contain and shape out of himself, of his ability to pit himself against obstacles. In this phase the sense of his will, the reach of his power, the pleasure of concentration are growing. And important above all is his feeling 'I can do it' which, established at this stage, will carry him throughout his life through many a difficulty but, if he does not achieve it then, will render him hesitant and fearful, even though the task be well within his capacity.

School-age hazards

Because this phase is so important, it is also of great danger when things go wrong. This may easily happen if the new developments are not guided in a way appropriate to the child's age, young strength and, above all, to his limited experience. These dangers depend a great deal on how he has been prepared for this stage, how he has reached the moment to step into school. For instance, the difference between the home and the school situation can be so great that the child may be shocked, feel different and isolated. Here can be the root of a later sense of being a misfit, the 'odd man out'. Instead of finding oneself wanted and valued as oneself, the child may feel he has to put himself on a shelf, abandon himself, comply once again with the expectations of others and force himself into a way which is too much at variance with himself. For example, if he cannot find his companionship with one or more of his fellows, his belongingness to a group among them or a good relationship to the teacher, and have the appropriate acknowledgment of himself from him, then he may be deflected from healthy adaptation into a pseudo-pattern such as trying to become the model pupil, the bright boy or girl. Others might feel rejected by the world of learning and because of special skills escape into games and become too one-sided and unbalanced that way, and a mind of great potentialities could thus lose the joy of learning.

The clown

To this group belongs the one which specialises in being the clown, the grotesque. It may all look very nice and cheery and hearty from the outside, but the agony, the distress can be unutterable. It is a terrible price to have to pay so as to win the necessary amount of belongingness, the price of a pseudo-life, and on a very narrow basis at that. Belongingness, the feeling of being wanted in some way or another, is essential especially for the young individual to survive and to feel his value, and so eventually answer this vital need from within himself.

Last but not least there are those unhappy children who escape from their difficulties by becoming the villains, the 'bad child', the one who makes a speciality of dirty stories or sexual information which gives them a feeling of having a place or meaning, a forbidden knowledge which the others want. So all these young children enter life as it were through a dark door, and only slowly, through some subsequent development, can light be brought to it.

Clinging to the group

Another danger that meets the ego is that of becoming dissolved in a group, of losing one's sense of identity, one's capacity for initiative. This occurs when the ego has not become rooted enough in itself, in the sense of its own significance, when in the previous phase the I–Me has been too often rejected and so not accepted as precious and unique by himself.

Here I would say that, up to a point, it is necessary to become committed to the group or to a gang, but if the identification goes on for too long, then the gang can become another womb, another maternal container which the ego is fearful to leave, to assert itself against even with those within the group.

Eternal schoolboy

There is, finally, the type of the eternal schoolboy. Damage occurring at such periods of crystallisation will tend to repeat itself and its pattern at each subsequent round of the spiral. We can observe this in the young adult who totally surrenders to a group, to an ism, to a party or, maybe, to a religious sect.

Will

So far we have not mentioned 'will', that is holding a purpose against resistance. This, of course, is a point of paramount significance, one of the decisive factors which have their formation at this period of purposeful acting and holding and serving a chosen aim or cause.

Anxiety and guilt

It is at this time that what we later call a chronic condition of anxiety may develop. It comes about because there is no constant reliable thread of security to relate the inner to the outer world.

There is no base to fall back on or firm line to orientate by, so a chronic state of fear, apprehension and guilt may develop.

We will pause for a moment to consider guilt. As a healthy reaction to wrongdoing it has its function and its rightful place. But without balance and if not used as a guide to insight and doing better next time, it can become one of the most crippling influences on the development of the ego. A latent feeling of guilt arises fundamentally from the child being brought up with too absolute conceptions of right and wrong, not related to a definite situation but generalised and made absolute — say absolute truthfulness, goodness or purity, and many others. 'Yes' and 'no', 'good' and 'bad' should serve life, protect it, facilitate it, yet if used in a blind moralistic sense, as principles standing in their own right and not linked up with a particular occasion or higher value to the young individual and his condition, they can be incalculably harmful. Here religious teaching comes in — the way it is mediated decides whether it can become a fruitful source of strength, or else something which later on the adolescent or adult may have to fight and reject, and then with great labour, if he is fortunate, find a new way to his own religious sense and expression.

As an example of the helpful or destructive application of religious conceptions we will take the attribute of God as the all-seeing one. As a protector, as the one who sees the danger and cares, who tells you the way, He will guide you through the darkness and the thunderstorms and the tempests. If mediated in the appropriate individual way, at the right moment and occasion, He can be an ever-present source of strength in times of trouble, a great reassurance. But if He becomes the one who finds you out if you look up forbidden words in a dictionary, go to bed without brushing your teeth and a thousand more things of this kind you have been told to do or not to do, then He can become a very interfering Almightiness, rather akin to the Devil, much hated and most feared.

In healthy conditions, however, this pre-puberty stage can be one of the happiest periods of life. Zestful and confident, not overshadowed yet by the confusions and bewilderments of the puberty period, not burdened yet by later responsibilities, with confidence in what the body can accomplish, in what the mind can see and find out, the child in a fortunate case goes forward with this compactness of personality into the next phase of puberty, in which new urges come rushing up from archetypal centres and flood him with feelings and imagery which he has only faintly and dimly experienced before, if at all.

The critical stage of puberty

Of this important stage of the personality shaping itself to its mature form, I will give two examples. The first is of a young girl who, introduced by an understanding mother, is experiencing her first menses as a token that the creative bloodstream of nature is now also streaming through her, that she is now included in it and able to hand on life to the next generation through her very body and being. The second is a quotation from the notes of a young man. At the age of twelve he experienced and observed his first erection. He looked at it with proud amazement, said to himself: 'This is something to show the boys,' and proudly strutted around the dormitory of his boarding school which at the moment was unoccupied. If this experience of personal pride in 'my life in my body' could by an initiation rite or a wise elder friend be connected with the sum total of creativeness which we call God, the biological expression of creativeness in him would for his lifetime be bonded to its spiritual counterpart. This could bring him close to the source of creativeness as expressed in the ritual of circumcision, in which the biological function is combined with spiritual meaning, a most important and significant coming together, one of the basic transcendent ones.

Painful aspects of puberty

The negative and painful aspects of puberty are only too well known to many of us. The blessing that the relationship between body and spirit can bring about may become a source of bewilderment, confusion, fear, apprehension and, sometimes, despair. Instead of relating to nature as a friend, it becomes too often a realm of failure, and will is pitted against nature which always in the end has the last word. Fighting this battle alone brings about an awful feeling of isolation, and so when others are found in the same predicament there may be a link-up. This may be a necessary transitional experience but, if lingered in too long, can become a static pool of frustration and despair out of which so-called homosexuality and lesbianism may become established. We must not forget that being guilty is often helpfully relieved by finding others in the same boat; but, unduly prolonged, this may bring about an arrest of development and a limiting, a blocking of the forward-goingness of the ego which eventually hopes to find an appropriate correspondence in the opposite sex.

This phase, ideally leading to the integration of body, mind and spirit, can, and so often does, easily become a splitting phase. A division starts, a gulf is fixed between body and heart, and body, heart and mind, so that the body stays earthbound in almost mechanical reflexes and gets mere short-term relief under those conditions. In those who are still sensitive to it, this leaves an unutterable sense of deprivation of heart and feeling and spirit, if their totality is not included. While the body becomes biologically determined, the heart, in a young man at least, may remain in the grip of his mother and her clinging possessiveness, whereas this phase is meant to be the great stimulus for his release and not castration.

Initiation rites

Here we realise so painfully the inadequacy, the poverty of our culture, of our social system. We miss the initiation rites which, with the help of mature guidance, enable the young adolescent to be freed from the natural maternal grasp and, by relating him to the spiritual lore of the tribe, help him forward into the realm of adulthood so as to become a full, individualised member of the community. All healthy tribes are related to the spirit of the ancestors and their great creation myth, and so the initiation rite relates the growing generation both to the ancestors and, through their creation myths, to God.

Modern society not only lacks this link between body, spirit and mind which the initiation rites of primitive societies still provide, but the Christian confirmation service gives its blessing only to the spiritual realm and depreciates the body in which the spirit has to dwell. The young adult, possessed with the full flowering of the body, is urged to what is called sublimation of the great creative force into spiritual expression.

In analysis, you meet the most agonised experiences of the age of puberty, when the conscientious and those of desperate loyalty to their upbringing try to shut out the body and etherealise it in spirit — of course, a completely impossible attempt for anybody of that healthy lusty age. The recurrent phrase of exhortation at that time is Serve God with a pure heart, but a valiant and often gallant attempt to achieve this makes the young heart, instead of pure, into a dungheap of frantic chaotic images, a turmoil of despairing, conflicting life urges.

This violation of nature is felt deeply and causes a great deal of disharmony and unhappiness. In the best of cases, youngsters will rebel and seek their own inexperienced way, the more over-whelmed ones are warped and damaged often for a lifetime, and it is from this group that we can get deep insight, in analysis, into the basic needs of this age. I think here of a man who had a dream in which he protested violently against God, and in the dream had a blackout. In association with it he remembered that once while at chapel in his school, a young fellow stood up and made a fervent protest, and subsequently the boy was removed from school.

In puberty we see most dramatically and desperately the struggle of the ego to assert and carry forward into life its archetypal values which as an individual it is called upon to mediate in his earthly life span. Here we find coming together a desperate urgency to discover, express and experience oneself and life, while at the same time breaking away from such traditional patterns as are felt to be cut and dried. Here we should distinguish between, on the one hand, a mere protest against inhibiting traditions and family ties and on the other, a real need of the individual, at least for the time being, to sever his relationship from father or mother or both, in order to have the fullness of his vital energy available to grow forward into his own adult way, to find his own meaning.

If the personality is fated to have an individual contribution to make, however great or small, we find in many a discoverer, inventor and pioneer it is around this period that their sense of vocation may come into awareness, that the germ is formed of the conception which throughout their lives they are going to give energy and time to express.

Struggle and regression

Here I wish to say a word about struggle. This is as two-sided as all other things which we deal with here, as Jung stressed time and again. Struggle in itself is not an aim, not a blessing. It can bring about growth, can mean destruction. The final aim is co-operation and not struggle, which should be a servant to the growth, to the life of the individual. One might even speak of a 'struggle neurosis' when the individual acts as if, in order to have a sense of existence and meaning, he must have a struggle; in very severe cases he will screen the surroundings and bring it about. If not appropriately dealt with and understood, this may lead to paranoia.

On the other hand, there are those who, giving up the struggle of relating to the outside world, regress entirely to the inner world and live in and with it. But for the eccentrics who manage to maintain themselves outside in isolation, we find them in the mental hospitals. Never forget that, although many may be unhappy in psychiatric clinics, there are some who have found their real home there and live in an ordered self-containment in which they fulfil themselves inwardly, even though they may not leave their mark and signature in outer reality. Could we say that in this situation the ego has found its place and its peace in identifying itself with the inner collective forces and figures of the great unconscious?

Lastly, there are those who go through an acute psychosis, a psychotic period, and may well come out of it with an enriched personality, with the experience of initiation.

I can in this context only hint at the further stages of ego development comparable to when the plant, previously sheltered, is planted out, when the ship goes out from the harbour into the open sea, exposed to the wind and the rain, and the sun that may or may not shine. There will be phases as important as those of learning and professional training, finding one's own line and work in the world, one's friends, one's marriage partner. There will come the richness and gathering of the second half of life when the more or less established maturity of the first half may need to reorientate anew, turning its primary energy from the ego to the self, discovering new wonders and values which tend to knit the total of life experience into the unity of a larger sphere.

IV

Healing in Depth

IV

THE CHILD WITHIN (1959)

In speaking about what I have called the child within, may I remind us of the significance of the child as an age-old symbol that carries with it, or evokes, in all who are in a condition to be moved by it, the sense of wonder, awe, hope, redemption, creative possibilities, the richness of becoming, of the future, the sense of adventure, zest, discovery, courage, spontaneity, undoubtedness, wholeheartedness and meaning—in other words all that the wise men felt when after their long intuitive journey, guided by their eternal star, they found the Christ Child. It brings with it the sense of individuality, eternity and immortality.

The child, as Jung's researches have found, is a symbol which has been experienced again and again in different eras from the earliest times of human history. In other words, it represents a crucial, age-old experience and hope of mankind which is ever with us yet ever young—one of the archetypal experiences—and therefore carries and evokes fascination and numinosity.

On the other hand, when the eternal image is seen in an earthly child, one must never forget that besides all the wonders there are also the little devils who at times can outwit the most sophisticated adult, especially when he, as it were, gets above his own nature; then, in an impish way, they may take control of the situation, quite amoral and irresponsible, and ruthlessly get what they want.

When I talk about the child within I mean that aspect within us adults which still reflects some of the qualities of the divine child, such as wholeheartedness, zest for life, awe and sense of wonder. When we are too unconscious of it, for whatever reason, and so do not mediate it, this force contains all the potentialities for constructive and destructive activities. So it can hold the creative dynamics of the human personality, its motive power.

From this we can realise how important it is to become aware of it, because then there is a chance to relate to it consciously and be reinforced by it and carried along without detriment to our adult judgments and responsibilities. Otherwise we may be unconsciously identified with it and thus be run, or our adultness even swamped, by its highly charged potential.

As a psychotherapist, however, one is confronted mainly with the difficulties of the child at various levels of its development in its environmental setting, in short with the problem child. We also find it within the adult patient, very often as the central core of his trouble and the disturbances that bring him to seek the therapist's help. In the adult, because of its usually early root and decades-old reaction pattern, it requires a deep analysis to trace this problem child inside oneself and bring it back into the stream of life. This is what I call healing in depth.

The stem of the personality

I would like now to introduce an image which helped me greatly in tracing and recognising such wounded aspects of the personality which in the course of treatment we hope to link up with, to restore and help to reintegrate within the total personality. I find it useful to look upon the personality as a stem in which every unit of time from birth to old age is represented, just as every season of a tree's life from its earliest sapling days is represented within its stem. In the case of the human being this stem can be thought of as crowned with the glow of consciousness of the present moment. To me this makes a vivid image of the spiral growth of a tree and the development of the psyche.

To continue with this image, the roots are sunk deep in the unconscious, the most recent ancestors closest to the beginning of the stem. At the base of the stem is the mother-child phase, and then comes the first budding of the child's individuality. At this early time the child's sense of himself reaches a certain definiteness; his differentiated consciousness begins to flower off from his unity with nature, his containment in the parents and in himself. It is a critical time of great sensitiveness, and in an ideal setting, acceptance and the warmth of parental love will bridge over from the early contained state to the more differentiated and less secure one which prepares the child for adult life. If the parents accept and affirm the value of his individuality and he can respond to this, the sense of his basic values becomes rooted and he will be able to make a more or less easy relationship with his environment into and from which he is growing. His experiencing

of a fair share of loving acceptance of his basic nature is fundamental to his healthy being and living. Then, with sufficient
security, he will go forward to the subsequent stages of development with the zest, self-confidence and sense of inner integrity
which are his birthright as a human being, and so the sap of his
energy will flow freely in his personality.

But if the parents, because of their own insecurity or for other
reasons, do not or cannot accept sufficiently his basic nature, or
if the child's inner or outer environment* is such that he cannot
receive enough of what he needs, then at this point where consciousness is so sensitive to the instinctual basis of being, his
personality may be severely damaged. Beyond the normal bruising,
he becomes estranged from his centre of being. Unknowingly he
feels forced to twist or even abandon his natural pattern of unfold-
ing, and by trial and error he learns a way of behaviour that is
more acceptable to his surrounding world, and which brings him
the acceptance and security he so badly needs. Here we have the
beginning of what may later become a very damaging distortion of
natural expression, a mental construction replacing natural relationship.

With the differentiation of consciousness, selectivity evolves
and certain aspects of his nature unacceptable to the parental
authority and environment are not allowed to be spontaneously
expressed. This kind of severe or repeated early experience lays
down a reaction pattern for subsequent phases. This may include
anxiety, apprehension and guilt, particularly when it comes to the
expression of his instinctual self and being. Because of the distortion of his personality he will doubt his own validity and basic
natural meaning. Consciousness gets out of tune with his nature,
and he may grow up, in part at least, at war with his basic self. I
call this area of damage, with such deep wounds in the personality,
the place of 'critical hurt'.

Types of traumatic experience

If now we turn to *types of traumatic experiences* I would distinguish between two different categories: *sudden and acute* on
the one hand, and *repetitive or recurrent* on the other. Before we
concentrate on those which have a deep-reaching or lasting effect
and which we can approach by means of psychotherapy, I would
like, for the sake of completeness, to pause for a moment to note
the fact that there are incisive experiences which do *not*, or need
not, have a damaging effect in later life. Having to go to hospital

*See above, p. 74.

for an operation may bring a traumatic experience to one child that calls for analytical treatment later on, but to another child, as I recently heard, it brought a reinforcement of his feeling of value and significance. Peter, aged six, previously indifferent to food and boyish games, came back radiant and rapidly became a robust little fellow. This remarkable transformation, which held its effect over several years, only revealed many years later during analysis, was that the surgeon after the operation called him a little hero and the nurses he felt had treated him as such. Again, one can readily see the difference between someone losing his leg by jumping from a moving bus or, say, at the battle of Alamein: the first may be damaged in his attitude to himself while, in the second case, the feeling of a hero may well increase his morale rather than lower it.

We might further differentiate between predominantly external, physical causes and internal, psychological ones. In both cases the effect depends first of all on the actual depth of the threat to health and life. It is of the utmost importance to separate that which is objectively and biologically traumatic and differentiate it from the subjective intensity of reaction which may be disproportionate to the objective data. Less severe cases, such as, say, a fall from a horse, a bite from a dog or violation by an adult, depend in the traumatic effect not so much on the event as such but on how it is experienced and dealt with, or whether and how it links up with an already existing pattern. A fall from a horse, to one, may reinforce his inferiority and lack of achievement, the other may lose his fears of falling by falling 'safely' without the fearsome result anticipated and increase his feeling of security. As you may know, in learning to ski you have to learn how to fall securely and get up again, on your very first day of tuition. Again, when stricken by polio, the extent of the trauma depends on the appropriate handling, for instance whether it is experienced as a challenge or as a punishment. I remember one stricken individual who, from his interest in movement arising from the damaged leg, became a good athletic instructor at a boys' school.

Still within the category of sudden and acute types of damage, I would like to point out that this extent has to be judged by whether the outer event produces a *sensitised critical area*, so that, whenever afterwards that area is activated, the response is that to the original threat and hurt. This may be very concealed so that ten to fifty or more years later, an apparently innocuous event may send the individual into a spasm of despair unexplainable by the actual context as such. The possibility of this reaching back to infancy may help us to get nearer to the realisation that an early trauma, even a birth trauma, may give the foundation from which a pathway of special sensitivity might extend up through the years into adult life.

We come now to the type of traumatic experiences which are caused not by a sudden, single or acute event but are brought about by a *sequence* of what in themselves would be minor experiences. I have found that it is rarely a single event but a *recurrent* everyday experience that may accumulate like certain drugs and become equivalent to a severe single trauma. So, in searching for damaging or traumatic agencies, it is necessary to look not only for the outstanding isolated trauma but for the influence of a demoralising atmosphere or milieu or inhibiting environmental conditions which one might call traumatically sensitising. As a steady drop of water may wear away a stone, so a repeated 'nag' can undermine the morale of the most stout-hearted child. If this influence is prolonged and effective through-out the growing period, then the child's development incorporates a pattern too divergent from his natural one for a healthy life.

Areas of critical hurt

My conception of healing in depth is based on a revaluation of the significance of unconscious areas of critical hurt. Occurring usually within the formative periods of growth, hurts are critical when the individual's instinctive nature, the feeling of himself, his sense of continuity, his image of himself, or essential values of his life have been damaged. I have found that such damage is to be looked for at a juncture where ego consciousness emerges from the instinctual matrix; this may occur at any of the budding phases. Such a buried wound in the personality results in block-ing the continuity of the flow of psychic energy within the stem of the personality up through all subsequent turnings of the spiral of growth. Areas of critical hurt create a blockage because, in order to hold the shock, the area is numbed off. At this moment vital units go, so to speak, off into limbo, the safe place of the unrecognised, the unaccepted, the rejected. In severe cases total amnesia may be the reaction because such a place of hurt is literally unbearable to consciousness, so unbearable that it is sometimes blacked out completely. To stand this strain, to pro-tect this most sensitive area, a kind of iron curtain comes down as a desperate device of self-protection and self-preservation. It is often made up of mentally developed coldness and objectivity towards oneself and frequently also towards others. Such imper-sonal coldness all too often indicates the guarding of an unbearable hurt, of insecurity, self-depreciation, loss of meaning and a sense of inferiority which if exposed would lead to overwhelming despair and panic.

Such areas of critical hurt, however, contain not only traumatic experiences which require attention but also have concealed energy within them, live energy that got blocked. This is energy of a particular kind, dawn energy close to the budding of a new phase of growth which, like nascent hydrogen, holds special power. Here suspended moments of time, instead of dying, by one of the wonders of nature and life, survive with all their potential energy and vitality, miraculously retaining, maybe for decades, their original specific charge.

Unfortunately, this energy is not available to the present-day personality who would need it badly. For these units of live energy are shut off, remain suspended in the shadow, cocooned parts of the earlier healthy personality. This cut-off area is not under the control of the ego, of the individual's will-power and consciousness, and has all the possibilities for good and evil which are a characteristic of the shadow area.

How, then, as they are so deeply concealed in the unconscious, can we know of them at all, relate to them, hope to modify them and get them out of their darkness, constructively back into the stream of life? These concealed dynamic centres are, as one might put it, sending out radioactive interferences. They exert a determining and often fateful influence, seemingly irrational and without cause, on subsequent phases of development right up to the present, especially on occasions which are highly personally charged. For the analyst, however, it is this trail of seemingly irrational occurrences that guides him in tracing the existence of such areas of critical hurt, assessing their depth, severity and prognosis and, beyond this, help him to map out, as it were, the patient's potential lifeline.

The patterns reflecting critical hurt situations tend to manifest themselves whenever there is a chance. I think of a very competent young woman doing excellent work who lost one job after another because unknowingly she created in the office setting a criss-cross of tensions reflecting her early unhappy family pattern. It was as if distorting lenses were interposed between her and the actual situation so that, despite her friendliness and efficiency, her colleagues instinctively resented her projection.

At the same time, you see here a clear example of how such areas of critical hurt come out as projections and thus can become recognisable with appropriate help. As a matter of fact, I could help this patient and several others in similar circumstances by relating their present-day calamity, for such it was, with the interfering reactions of their deep-seated damage.

On the other hand, the feeling of distress caused by such recurrent, apparently irrational interferences can bring about a sense of urgency that will lead the sufferer to seek the help which psychotherapists try to bring.

As an example I have chosen one from this recurrent repetitive type of traumas: the child under the influence of an atmosphere emanating from the relationship of the parents.

Mrs. Somerset

Mrs. Somerset, as we will call her, a woman of seventy-one years, mother of a daughter and a son, whom I had seen many years ago for analysis, wrote for an interview. Two years previously she had consulted a psychiatrist who after the first interview told her that nothing could be done for her. When she arrived, her complaints were feelings of inferiority for many years, an inexplicable tenseness and short, fluctuating moods of well-being and depression since her marriage forty years ago or so. Her husband had died after the Second World War, and a few years later she nursed her dying mother for several months till her death. After a trip around Africa and back in England she had settled down to living with her son and his family in the depth of the country. She had come to feel that she was going to seed, and at times even the beautiful landscape outside looked dead and as if made of cardboard. One asks oneself here: this is a serious symptom — how deep does it go? This sign of depersonalisation was in strong contrast with the natural vividness, vitality and colourfulness of the woman sitting opposite me. She had even become ashamed of visiting friends because she felt so old and unattractive; a naturally slim figure, she had recently also been losing weight.

Before Mrs. S. wrote for an interview to me she had been struggling for several weeks to make up her mind as to whether to come for a consultation or not, hoping, as she said, to be able to do it all herself — a not uncommon error to fall into: the one who originally suffered from lack of appropriate parenting now hesitates to accept much-needed help. In the past few months she had had a series of stressful experiences, losing not only a lifelong woman friend but also a near relative. Moreover, her daughter-in-law had been threatening to leave her son, and her daughter was getting a divorce after nine years of marriage with two children. She herself had developed arthritis of the hip which suddenly limited her mobility and, as she said, made her feel quite ancient; however, a thorough medical check-up had found her very healthy for her age.

Frequently, the first dream one takes to one's analyst is of central significance. In a similar way, I take special notice of how a patient introduces himself or herself at the first interview. Mrs. S. did so by thanking me for having helped her daughter years ago to find and develop a latent gift for painting (by the way, after overcoming a strong resistance against drawing, with the help of spontaneous doodling) and to become a professional artist, and also for helping her son who had told her: 'It was Dr. Barker who enabled me to live with myself.'

Apart from seeing how well she had stood up to having both children growing away from her, I took her self-introduction as a possible hint that she had a hope to develop a latent talent of her own on the one hand and, on the other, to strive towards living on better terms with herself.

As her stay in London was limited, I had only a few sessions to assess what one might call her basic make-up and potentials, to see how her inborn pattern was distorted, how far she had been able to live it out and to what extent the picture and feeling of herself had been damaged by the limitations both of her environment and of herself; and, finally, to help her to link up with, relate to and value this inborn pattern and live from it. That is, to recover both her self-respect and her morale, recognise her natural potential self, become friendly with it and live from this rather than from the distorted picture.

The question was how this could be achieved, and in such a short time?

First, one listens and gives attention to the immediate worries and troubles which are uppermost, because only when these have been lightened and, as far as possible, attended to, can the mind be free to go deeper. In her case, the situation, for instance, with her children, had to be seen in perspective and burdens of responsibility shed which did not really belong to her. Attending constructively to the guilt feelings as they came up, I had to help her to let her children, now parents themselves, go their own way and, with the energy thus released, take up more maturely the needs of her own life.

Although attending to the immediate needs first, from the very beginning I look out for any detail or experience that reflects the healthy inborn pattern and the way the individual has come up through life, with the aim of eventually being able to view them in my mind from the present adult in front of me down through the corridor of the growing years to their undisturbed original self. The picture of the way the patient has come has to be built up bit by bit and is not to be forced into an ordered sequence as if one was making out a formal report. For it is essential that one follows and encourages the spontaneity, so that the words can come from the depths of their very being and truth.

Mrs. S.'s life story may serve as an example of a handicapping reaction pattern that arose principally from what one might call a chronic traumatising atmosphere, largely from the parental relationship. Both parents were brilliant individuals in their own right, the mother was an artist, a sculptress in fact — very unusual in these later Victorian times; the father, a professional man, had retired early to become a scholar and writer on mathematics. Each of the parents was thus highly endowed, but evidently the marriage was never bonded on a deep instinctual level. All the members of this family seemed to maintain themselves in a rather strange, peculiar separateness from each other: the mother in her studio, the father in his study, and the children — there was an older brother — each building up their own little world. But it was as if the atmosphere for my patient lacked some vital stimulus or hormone, might we say, that would bring forward the dormant abilities to develop, especially marked in the critical phase of puberty to adultness. Thus I was not surprised to hear when she quoted her mother as saying that the only drawback that blotted the happiness of her marriage was to be expected to have sexual intercourse. No wonder, then, as she herself said about her later teenage, that she was emotionally very backward in development. In her own words, 'like a tightly closed bud', although in other respects she was healthy, happy at school and enthusiastic and good at sports and swimming; up to sixteen she had a very good friend, an Italian girl, and missed her much when she went back to Rome.

Although a normal pre-puberty girl, she was as if something prevented her from opening out and allowing for the teenage flow of sexual stirrings and urges, so that even under the most favourable conditions when the young woman met the ideal young man, these did not take place.

'At twenty-one', she told me, 'I was introduced to a gifted and musical family, which included a young man of my own age, and together with him the beauty of the world opened up to me. But in looking back now I realise how strange it was that, when he kissed me, although I did enjoy it, there was no deep bodily stirring.'

We have here a puzzle such as, by the way, I found in other families even nearer to our time, in which the children have loving care and apparently everything they need, but still there must be something seriously wrong of a very basic kind. In Mrs. S.'s life this 'something' kept her in the pre-puberty stage, which apparently was a rich and happy one. The parallel between the parental relationship and her own inability to respond to her young man with whom she shared so much and, finally, her inability to reach later, in her marital relationship, total fulfilment, made me wonder and ask about what was wrong in the picture, possibly apart from, and additional to, a more usual fixation on the father.

And then, how did it link up with the similar contradiction of this well-preserved woman, with surprising aliveness at seventy-one complaining about the feeling of deadness she experienced at times when looking into a beautiful landscape and feeling as if it were of cardboard? I had to find out whether this was inborn or there were circumstances that could account for it. At first I was not at all sure which. With no evidence of cyclothymic swings before her marriage, I dared to come to a tentative conclusion that here indeed we had met a case of the effect of traumatising surroundings on a healthy, gifted and naturally passionate nature. Could it be that the very thing that was meant to give her new impetus for life, carry her forward and lift her up, would make her feel depressed and inferior? Had she, held under the negative parental approach to deep spontaneous expression, particularly on the instinctual level, so to speak unconsciously felt guilty and inferior, taking this as her own, personal and individual inferiority and shortcomings? Could it have been, then, that all her parents' giftedness had been one-sidedly and perhaps desperately canalised into so-called sublimation, in the studio of the one and in the study of the other, so that these became not only the place of artistic expression but the burial place for basic creative fusion of body and mind?

To cut the story of over fifty years short: the *leitmotif*, the guiding theme, was the negative auspices under which she had lived, viewed and evaluated her own life experience and achievements, and that falling short of a rightful sense of zestful fulfilment, the effect of the traumatic inhibition of her surroundings, was mistaken as her personal insufficiency.

In the few times I saw her we reviewed, reactivated as it were, the salient features of her life, developing in detail critical places, events and relationships and judging how far these showed either an inhibiting effect on her natural self or revealed the full expression of it. Her experience as a young girl was repeated in her marriage which, although she enjoyed sexual intercourse, did not stir her deeply enough to give her a total fulfilment: she never had an orgasm.

She had married without deep feeling, having met her husband who was five years older, during the First World War. He was quite persistent over several years and she finally gave in, more from reasoning, and married him while on leave from the front. Incidentally I happened to have met her husband; he was unusually nice but inhibited in his spontaneity—was that the possible link with her father? After an army career he became an education officer in the R.A.F. and rose to a high position; he sacrificed his life to this vocation and died from overwork. I found it remarkable that when their son wished to become an actor—which certainly was an attempt to break out of the family pattern of emotional inhibition, as later on he became a farmer and then took up teaching science— the father, though he did not like it, put no obstacles in his way.

When they had been married a good many years, her husband was stationed in another country, and they were separated for three months while he tried to find a house there. She recalled that these three months were a tremendous relief to her: everything became more vivid, she could relate more spontaneously and her natural joyfulness came out. It seems as if she lived with her husband in the inhibiting atmosphere of a deeply unconscious incestual relationship to her father, thus re-creating the old family pattern, without any awareness that it was a reflection of her early traumatic experience calling for recognition and release.

While she was with her husband, who was stationed in Egypt, one of the senior army officers asked whether she would come for a drive with him around the pyramids. Her husband did not mind. She went, and her companion said that he was very attracted by her— could he kiss her? She allowed it but did not feel anything. Later on, back in England, she reconsidered the incident and felt that she might quite have liked a relationship with that man. I saw in this half-heartedness yet another instance of the incestual pattern.

Her greatest stirring at depth took place when at forty-five she met another man, the age of her father. He was a doctor, and outwardly the relationship was kept within strictly professional bounds. But there was a tremendous rapport. She said that a sense of life and warmth came to her—it was as if a serpent uncoiled from around her heart. Any sexual relationship or external response was out of the question, but one day she asked him whether she could kiss him on the forehead, which he allowed. When she spoke about this relationship, her eyes were full of tears before she had time to control herself.

From this time onwards her marriage, up to her husband's death, was more satisfactory. Even after his death, on her trip round Africa when she was over sixty-five, one of the ship's officers, while she was looking at the notice board, put his hands on her hips and told her that he was very attracted to her. They had long talks in his cabin, and it helped her to realise that she was still an attractive woman.

She expressed the wonder that, in trying to recall these events when previously remembering them, she had not felt them so vividly, so meaningfully. It was of great importance that it revealed her need for an understanding consciousness which, in this instance, she found in the analyst.

Important as all her statements were, and particularly when the expression of feelings came up spontaneously, it was first in my deduction from these that I put together a very tentative image of her unlived life pattern, knowing all the time that I worked with a hypothetical concept of her potential self, on which I kept checking whilst she told me her life story. One may say that I painted from her own account a translucent picture through which she could recognise, as though in a magic mirror, the still distorted image of her potential self together with her shadow. It was reassuring that when I quite tentatively applied this possibility in connection with the events and the almost recurrent pattern of her life, it made sense not only to me but also immediately to her. One could say that analysis under the auspices of the entelechy of the individual is one in which one is guided by the golden thread, as it might be called, that relates the individual to his or her centre of being, and through that, to what one is meant to be.

In going through her life history, I could see that she was of a deeply passionate nature. But I could also understand that throughout her life she was burdened by a feeling of inferiority because she *lived* inferior to her natural capacity. The deep sense of inadequacy to nature from an early age arose out of the parents' relationship. If one has to humiliate and repudiate the basis of life, then one carries a burden throughout the expression of it. This indicated to me that there was a considerable amount of repressed spontaneous emotion, which confirmed several observations in the same direction.

The review, the inner re-experiencing of her life's journey up to the present, was used to emphasise and estimate wherever possible her wide potentialities and frequent achievements, often under very restricting circumstances, showing the rich glow there was under a very restrictive or shadowed outer life.

It helped and healed by enabling the patient to truthfully realise that, in various circumstances of life where she felt she had been impotent or inferior in a situation, she was potentially fully endowed, and because we were speaking to the truth and also had analysed the circumstances of how it came about, both her intellect and feeling could grasp and accept this reassessment of herself. So this part of her distorted or repressed image could be restored into its rightful form and beauty. And as this quality of realisation of different talents, both with her mind and feeling, was extended to other aspects of herself, one could see it reflected in the radiance of her face.

She thus regained her rightful self-respect by becoming aware that the root of many of the experiences which she put down to inferiority within her essential self, actually arose out of circumstances over which she had no, or at most only partial, control.

We remember that during the first interview I had gathered that she came with a barely concealed hope to develop a latent talent of her own and to learn to live on better terms with herself. In fact, it had always been her wish to become a writer, with some success, and this she now found the confidence to go forward with. We may ask in what way she is now better able to use her potential talents and gifts. Being more released from the distorting pull of the traumatising parental atmosphere, on the mother's side from the doubts of life's meaning in its earthly aspects and, on the father's side, from the inhibiting unconscious incestual relationship, will free her to be guided by her own creative power, her animus, and to express herself out of the fullness and truth of her life and nature.

As to her other hope to become better able to live with herself, she now has resonances of feeling which were previously muted, and being linked up with her meaning and thus, with her lifeline, will indeed enable her to do so. As a matter of fact, she is looking for a flat, away from her children and nearer to friends of her own.

A letter I received several weeks after the last interview confirmed that her new attitude and confidence in life was holding.

THE CRITICAL HURT IN THE VOCATIONAL FIELD

Becoming more and more aware of the significance of a critical hurt, I was struck to find outstanding examples of it in the field of vocation. It impressed me deeply that people who followed a vocation to which they gave a lifetime of energy and devoted attention, and who one would have thought would have obtained satisfaction, buoyancy and health from it because it was received and honoured by their colleagues and contemporaries, on the contrary found themselves exhausted, barren, sterile and despairing, to the point of suicidal thoughts. That was where I found them, bogged down in the vocational field. The very word 'vocation' rang a bell in me. Vocation is a *call*, and as defined in the dictionary, has the element of a *divine* call.

That surely meant that the call had come not from some whim of consciousness, some intellectual idea, but from a source much more vital, something springing from the main lifeline or core of the personality. In severe cases, the inability to obtain inner satisfaction from their vocational work was even leading to the hope of finding peace in the embrace of death.

The question then was: where did the vital call or challenge of vocation come from? This put me on the alert to look out for any hints towards an answer. I saw that, say, the social worker would become interested in certain types of cases, to some of which he would devote far more time and energy than he reasonably should, at the expense of his own personal life or of those to whom he was most personally connected, as for instance, a man to his wife or the wife to her husband or their children. Here, evidently, was a call or a need that went very deep indeed.

The term vocation was taken originally in relation to a religious experience in answer to a call from within. And, although I use it in a narrower psychological sense as an answer to the call from the place of critical hurt, I would like to apply it also in a wider sense. I believe all human lives are either an answer, or an attempt to answer, a deep necessity of their being, of their total psyche. Life, however lived, stems from a centre of being, a core beyond the ego and therefore can be called vocational, that is directed towards the divine, towards one's star, one's destined fate.

Just to give you some examples that have occurred in my work and that of a colleague who also applied and tested this conception of the original hurt and its relationship to vocation:

Repeatedly it was found that, in their work, psychiatric social workers, probation officers, house mothers for children in need of protection and care, were answering their own original hurt. They were giving to others what was not given to them at dawn time when they needed it, with the effect that they gave too much of their energy so that finally, illness brought them to analytical treatment and, with this, to the discovery and the rescue of their own starved and shut-off selves.

Another group where this relationship between vocational work and early hurt is often found, is among people who go into the legal profession. A solicitor especially known for the care and compassion with which he dealt with the distressing circumstances of divorce, was himself shut off from his own inner personal sensitiveness. In his profession he could deal, and most successfully, with the intimate problems of others while remaining 'objective' and detached himself.

Another example is a woman lawyer who fell in love with the husband of her best friend and had several pregnancies by him aborted; she ultimately decided that her friendship with the wife was more important to her than being in love with the man, her friend's husband. She gave up the relationship with him, feeling (rightly, as it turned out) that he would soon find another woman outside his very complicated marriage situation. But she herself gave up the practice of law, and after the necessary training, became a qualified midwife. In this way she indirectly gave birth and care to many hundreds of children, thus easing the pains of guilt she suffered for the feeling of having sinned against Life that her aborted pregnancies had given her. Later, after psychological treatment, she was able to build up a very satisfying relationship with a man appropriate to her maturing personality and did wonderful work in a more detached and less self-consuming way.

Then I recall an almost paradoxical choice of vocation by a woman who was unrelated to her instincts: she had hated the lower part of her body from childhood onwards. She became a gynaecologist and a successful pioneer in the field of birth control and artificial insemination.

Another, distressing, example is that of a young woman who was in love with the husband of her sister and became pregnant by him. She did not allow the child to come to term but had an abortion. The man committed suicide. After a time of utter despair, she conceived the idea of helping unwanted children. She collected sufficient money to found a home for them which she ran, and so gave to these children what she could not give to her own.

All these unhappy people eventually came for treatment because the original hurt was acted out—outside—and not dealt with appropriately from within.

Finally, I want to mention some material that has been personally recorded in detail by someone caught in this dilemma long before modern psychology and psychotherapy were available. For it satisfies the scientist in us if the conscious and unconscious material used comes from a person that cannot have been influenced either by analytical ideas or by the analyst in his field of interest. I mean *Florence Nightingale*, where the relationship between vocation and the original hurt is most striking. Coming from the rich, smooth life of nineteenth-century gentry, from a family background which she felt 'divided her asunder, soul from spirit, bones from marrow', she undertook to reform the nursing services out of her own critical hurt. From her inner loneliness she knew how it felt when nearness was needed most. Thus, in the Crimean War, she would always sense the place of greatest isolation, be with the man whose leg was amputated without anaesthetic, sit by the side of the dying soldier—doing for others what she felt excluded from in her own early life.

Tracing the original hurt

The conception of the critical hurt areas can lead to a short-cut diagnostic tracing of the chief interferences with the lifestream. After getting the patient at ease and establishing the necessary rapport as we always try to do, I am on the alert for signs of an interrelation between the difficulties of today with moments of comparable emotion and hurts in the past. In listening to the patient's story, one takes the present situation as potentially symptomatic, as a surface expression of something possibly much deeper. I look for a relationship between the patient's recurrent difficulties of today, with special attention to his type of work and its vocational significance, and an earlier unresolved difficulty or pattern. In other words, we allow for the difficulty of today to be constellated by a specific, unhealed, recurrent problem of the past—an *area of critical hurt*. In such cases the present-day situation happens to mirror more or less an earlier one that critically challenged the individual. It induced a defence reaction (including repression) which at the time saved the situation. This became habitual but, now in adulthood, no longer serves the individual's life.

It is most likely that the *deep hurts* that affect subsequent periods may have this *critical* quality *because the disturbing event coincided with the emergence of a basic human, an archetypal, situation or tension* at a moment of growth.

In checking on the importance and severity of this hurtful event or experience, by keeping one's ear very close to the message of dreams, including early nightmares and phantasies as well as of fears, apprehensions and feelings of guilt, one may well discover the same imprint or pattern in earlier or later events of the patient's life. Such recurrence points to the deep-seated critical hurt (the first one spotted is not necessarily the original one). *I am often guided to areas of critical hurt by the fascination exerted by their reflection* in a present person or situation.

This scanning, checking and assessing helps to trace the patient's injury right through the years to the present as well as the complexes involved and constellated. By noting and feeling the type of reaction that he brings to stress situations — for instance that of the withdrawing schizoid, the victim paranoid, the hysterical or the obsessional type — we get a quickened sense of the diagnosis.

Out of this specially sensitive anamnesis we can judge some *factors essential for assessing the possibility and type of treatment and the prognostic outlook.* I would emphasise the health and quality of the patient's substance; the stamina of the personality, its resilience or brittleness; the effort and persistence put into reaching the unconscious, and its response to it. Next I would mention the importance of environmental factors and their impact, in particular on the hurt area and the shaping of the defence pattern. Of equal importance for regrowth where possible is the integrity of the ego, however young and immature it may be in the adult of today, and his capacity to mature in due course and take over responsibility, not only for his outer but also for his inner life. In the external reality I would check the degree of security in the environment, the range of experience and daring independence, the counterpoise in work, in the family, with friends, the rootedness in their own sex and the healthy relationship to the opposite, and lastly, I would estimate the degree of isolation.

The comparatively early or late occurrence of the critical hurt area, the degree of health underneath it, the more or less complicated reaction pattern built over the wound may help to establish an *early tentative prognosis* as to chances of 'cure', to assess the type of therapy, the probable duration and frequency of treatment indicated.

Altogether, my concern ranges *from the dilemma of today down to the original hurt and back again* — a span that is radioactive, as it were, in a complex psychological sense in its influence on the present day. My conception provides *an additional means*, a ray that may guide us more directly to such critical areas. Together with the many other aids of analytical psychology, it *gives an added wavelength* or special beam to the therapist engaged in such pioneering endeavours.

The necessity for a careful anamnesis, the tracing of the life pattern, has always been recognised, but in my opinion the critical incidents in the childhood of the patient are often not appreciated in their full significance, let alone *consciously* reconnected with the healthy younger part of the personality, hidden before the hurt and, even if recognised, these healthy components of the personality are allowed to recede too soon into the background. In my experience they need a continuity of daily care, as children do. Moreover, they tend to be treated in analysis too often as something in the historical past rather than living energetic parts of the present adult personality which, although unconscious, are continually exerting their influence. No profound healing can take place until they have been brought back, may have decided to come back, have seen they are wanted, that now at last it is safe to come out once more. When this has been proved again and again, tested out time after time under varying conditions, they return into the flow of the circuit of life and, as it were, participate in it and are fed back by daily helpful incidents—maybe by the very 'food' that the patient is giving to others in his or her devoted work.

The task in general is to enable the adult of today, burdened with a life-restricting pattern, to reach such insight and capacity as will enable him to give to the area of critical hurt that parental care whose absence brought his pattern into being. As it has had its reflection through every phase up to the present, one can learn to recognise it at different ages, not only in the abreaction, in discussing events of the past, but also in spotting different age reactions in the person of today. For instance, the middle-aged professional man may in one moment respond as an enthusiastic teenager and in another as the naive little boy he was before the hurt.

Very special care and personal attention are needed in this particular work. For, going to places of critical hurt of a severe nature reproduces all the tensions of life and death of those original childhood moments when, to save itself, some part of the personality had to go into limbo, the half-way house between earth and heaven. When these are constellated and activated in the adult, the suicidal tendencies of the moment are also activated—without the possibility of falling into oblivion, that safe place available and reachable to the hurt child. It needs the utmost awareness and clearness of the analyst, and his steadiness, especially when his own place of hurt is activated, to provide the sensitiveness and continuity of support that is required (1) to prevent isolation, panic and suicide and (2) to guide the released energy towards answering the need and life problem of the patient's here and now.

The importance of this close and continuous attention to the actual situation cannot be overestimated: it gives these precariously balanced patients some much-needed earth under their feet.

James

We will now draw on the analysis of a young man to illustrate the tracing of the original hurt which helped me to reach the disturbed area in a short time and enabled him to make a crucial life decision.

James is a man in the early thirties, a university teacher. He came to consult me because he was in a state of uncertainty, tension and panic about getting married, the date having been fixed; in fact, six weeks was the exact time. He was sent to me by a woman colleague because she felt that he needed a man to help him on and the time was running short.

He had originally come to analysis about eighteen months before, as he sensed that his academic work had become stale; although a good teacher because of his personal qualities, he feared that his creative writing (he was writing a book) had really dried up — 'non est', as he put it.

A short time after commencing analysis, he had met a girl, quite suitable, fell in love and was engaged six months later, and it was this which really set things going.

When he then came to see me he told me that, up to the age of twenty-eight, when he met this young girl, he had never had a relationship with a woman, he had no experience of sexuality. 'All my sexuality had been in masturbation,' he said. A few weeks before, he and his fiancée had attempted sexual intercourse but it was a fearful flop. He explained: 'From the first I was hopelessly split up by Victorian sexual taboos, and when in the early part of our engagement she offered her virginity, this was too much for me all at once.'

'The engagement,' he went on, 'was broken off for several months and then we again started to see each other, but her contact with some other men in the meantime haunted me; whenever I approached her I felt their presence around. She told me I was not a man like she had met last summer, and I saw his photo in her room. I became obsessed by the fact that my fiancée had known three men, and my father in me condemned utterly this behaviour, and not only hers but me for mine. I condemned her for her loss of virginity, but still cared tremendously for her. Both of us wanted each other.'

We went into his childhood memories, and he told me: 'My whole family situation is not a very happy one. At the age of nine I felt a very great concern because father and mother had a big row, and father cleared off to a hotel. I told Mother to write to Daddy and say: "Daddy, we want you back desperately, and *we* promise to be good."'

He felt strongly that 'Mother and Father pulled against each other, and I was pulled between the two.' In the tension and struggle between his parents, he took, in general, his mother's side—that is, he linked up with his mother against his father.

The close relationship to his mother on this deep level we might call in Jung's words 'the young mother-lover archetype situation'. He got an awful shock when he heard at school how children are conceived and born. To use his own words: 'When I found out how babies were born, instead of being interested I felt "how terrible!"'

From the notes I have of this time in his life, the early stage of the puberty phase, I know that this shock fired his phantasies, so that he became altogether afraid of phantasy stories. With his wakened-up interest in the mystery of sexuality and the male/female relationship, he began to search through his mother's cupboards and drawers and when he was twelve he found a letter showing that she had a lover: 'that my mother was unfaithful to Father was a tremendous shock to me'. It activated him violently, and he became partly identified with the father or, alternatively, with the lover figure, so much so that when his mother was pregnant again, he exclaimed to her: 'What will Daddy say?' As a matter of fact, his father said to his mother when he had made her pregnant: 'That will keep you bloody well quiet for a time.'

We recall that, after some weeks of analysis by a colleague of mine, this young man was able to fall in love with a very appropriate young girl, and was accordingly engaged half a year later. I mentioned the strange wording of his response to a great gift when his fiancée offered him herself as a virgin, 'her virginity was too much for me', and that when they met again and decided to marry, he was obsessed by seeing in his phantasy the men she had associated with—he became afraid of his own potency, his manhood. I evaluated, translated and linked up the two critical moments of his life in the following way.

Being a young boy, loving his mother, he felt guilty towards his father; and even before he became aware that his mother had a lover, his curiosity set him on the trail of finding the love letter that confirmed it. Thus, when he found out that his mother had 'another' lover apart from him—he himself being in his phantasy her lover—he felt violently outraged.

From then onwards he lived under the spell of the guilty, forbidden, mother-lover-son relationship. When he met his fiancée, he was unable to accept her as his wife-to-be because of her virginity, which prevented him from inwardly phantasying her as his mother. That is, he did not feel adequate to the present-day situation: to experience, as his next-needed step in the development of his own life, his own woman and not, as a son-lover, his mother.

When, therefore, fortunately or unfortunately, his young girl, after breaking off the engagement, had another man, it fitted his original situation perfectly; he had, so to speak, brought about the setting of his first inner experience of man-woman relationship, which was the incestuous one to his mother. The natural reaction of his healthy body answered this by impotence. It said 'No' to his mother, visualised in the girl.

You see, this is one of the situations in which one can become aware of the call of the original hurt area to make itself known by a *disturbance*, thus bringing about, through a present-day, here and now, *vital crisis situation*, a chance of being recognised and thus of being released and, finally, healed.

I felt strongly that the intensity of James's state mirrored the desperate situation of the young boy of nine and twelve with regard to his father and mother and the lover. I could grasp that the pattern of the conflict he was in today reflected the utter agony which that young boy of nine to twelve had gone through in relationship to his parents.

When I realised this, it was as if a spark flashed across the gap, across the decades, between the critical area of hurt in the lower stem of his psyche up through the spiral of time to the present moment, relating the dilemma of today with the original situation creating the difficulty James was wrestling with. This insight, carefully conveyed to him, brought a flood of clarity and meaning to him.

I may mention here that the effectiveness of these crucial insights, as I have seen them, depends not only on the facts linked together. It is at least as important that they are conveyed to the patient in an atmosphere of confidence and relationship which is charged with the problem and sensitised to it, with analyst and patient working together on clarifying and bringing help to a desperate human need.

When James had been able to relive this traumatic experience in the security of my consulting room, I could gradually help him to feel with growing awareness the astounding interrelationship between his present situation and his boyhood experience which had been so vital and shaking. This culminated in releasing and freeing him sufficiently to go forward into his next phase of life and marry at the appointed date.

More in general, when a deep critical hurt can be traced and linked up with a present crippling handicap, it is as if an estrangement is healed, as if long separated people who belonged to each other, lost for decades, suddenly find each other; it is a moment of deep meaning and a sense of linking up of the personality, an experience akin to a religious reunion—in fact, a lost, estranged portion of the soul has become related to, reunited.

I should like to add here an additional observation. Since writing the above, it has been astonishing how often the material that the patients have been bringing, at a particular moment in their analysis, has at the same time been helpful in illustrating my idea. I was quite struck by this when one afternoon, after I had been working all morning on James's material, thinking I could have done with some more details, he actually called me, long-distance, and asked if he could come up from the country to see me in London. I had not heard from him for six weeks—not since he married. And so he came, and we both, I hope, got what we needed. You will understand that all this brought me very close to Jung's observations on synchronicity.

The conception of areas of critical hurt versus reductive analysis

I would like to add the following general remarks about the tracing of such deep-seated injuries. The necessity for an anamnesis has always been accepted, but in my opinion the critical incidents and constellating environmental patterns in the childhood of the patient are often not seen in their full significance and extent, let alone the necessity to reconnect where possible the adult with the healthy younger part of the personality. Even if recognised, such units are allowed to recede into the background instead of being carried forward. Altogether they tend to be treated predominantly, almost exclusively, as aspects of the historical past rather than as living energetic parts of the present adult personality on which, although unconscious, they are continually exerting their influence.

If this situation is handled by superficial analysis, inappropriate interpretation, will-power or so-called rehabilitation, a certain amount of adaptation may be achieved. Two decisive factors, however, will be amiss: (i) the patient is working against the tension potential of his basic instinctual pattern, and so undue energy and will-power are required to operate such adaptation; and (ii) the original pattern in the depth, because never related to consciously by the mind nor feelingly by the heart, remains essentially unmodified. Hence it is ever ready to overcome, to swamp the new adaptation with an uprush of revengeful, repressed instinctual energy.

THE CONCEPTION OF FEED-BACK

The term 'feed-back' is taken from electronics. There it is the term used for a process in these new giant electronic calculating and sorting machines, in which masses of variegated information are stored, arranged and sorted in batteries of electronic cells. When the investigator wants a particular piece of information, he sends out a signal to the machine which scans the whole field and selects material according to the call that has been sent out. This is electrically collected and then fed back to the enquirer. Thus, we have an outgoing arc to the field of information and a returning arc, the *feed-back*, to the place from which the call for information went out, the place of need. When I came across this term in this connection, the imagery seemed to convey my idea of a psychological feed-back quite neatly.

The modern use of these giant electronic machines in what is called cybernetics seemed to mirror in a rather striking way the picture I have of the connection between the vocational field in the present here and now, and the circuit back from it to the place of original hurt. In both cases there is a circuit. The outgoing arc from an underlying place of injury we can readily understand and visualise. The stimulus of the need is sent out to where information is in probability stored, for instance in the vocational field of one's life work. Unless there is the return arc, back to the place of call, energy accumulates in outer reality, whereas the damaged area is waiting in vain for an answer. This explains the desperate tension that piles up in the field of work and, once recognised, the relief when the connection is made. The psychological aspect of this return arc would be what I call the *feed-back*.

As I mentioned before, I have come to realise that this feeding back of life experience to the area of original hurt really contains the whole *raison d'être* of the life work of many professional people. The tragic and dangerous dilemma in which these worth-while persons, devoted to their work, find themselves is, on the one hand, the caring for and feeding of others, on the other, the starving and killing of themselves, with the result that they feel their life becoming increasingly meaningless to themselves. The reason for this dreadful paradox I found in the link which was missing between the vocational field and the place from which the call initially came, the impoverished area which marks the point of original hurt. Hence the living energy of the experience and insight spent on others has to be fed back to the place of origin, the area of critical hurt, often of deepest personal significance. It is to this vital return arc that we now have to direct our attention and devotion. With its restoration, the lost personalness of such hurt people gains the possibility of being restored, for then they themselves can become included in their daily life; they are no longer an object, a tool in the service of others, working with an often self-destroying abnegation.

When I become thus tuned in, searching through the field of vocational activity, I scan the various areas of the psyche, down through the spirals of the personality, back to the earliest memory records, until I finally find an area of critical intensity corresponding to the pattern that had developed.

I then try to activate this special area by all the means available — dreams, active imagination, associations and transference — and linking up any experience in everyday life, be it in work or leisure, anything the patient hears over the wireless, sees in a theatre or film, reads in a newspaper or novel, that is of special significance to him — in fact, one keeps a constant watch on the whole field of conscious life, as well as what becomes available through the unconscious.

I am on the lookout for anything which produces an effect positively or negatively, i.e. either joyfully or fearfully. If this happens, then I know it has induced a response in the unconscious, as if a particular tuning-fork had been struck. And this is where I go, consciously, with as much care and sensitiveness as I can summon, to activate this area of answering resonance in the depth, and then relate the patient's conscious here and now to these living suspended moments in his depth, often decades ago. This process of relating the present to the place of original hurt or significant need, this building of the second part of the arc is what I call the *feed-back*.

An example of feed-back

A striking example of the efficacy of the *feed-back* came to me quite recently. A woman in her forties had had her life dislocated at the age of fifteen by the death of her father. He had mediated for her her whole security and personal valuation, as the mother relationship was negative and colourless. The patient was compelled by her unconscious to undertake the exacting and somewhat perilous task of re-relating with that unlived part of her personality, the late teenage young woman, which had to be suspended and, as it were, remained in limbo throughout the succeeding decades of her life. She became a most efficient and successful business woman, but to those who could discern it, with a severe lack on the feeling side. She was also a very courageous woman. When, after a year or two of analysis, which was very strongly supported by figures in the unconscious, she got near the fateful area down in the stem of her personality, she experienced pain in the solar plexus region. This was so severe that, had it been of a physical cause, such as gall stones, morphia would have been indicated. This pain had been going on intermittently for some months but recently had become most severe.

Pondering one day on this, I thought: 'This is of such persistence and intensity, it must be connected to the critical hurt,' the centre of which we were now very close to; she had recently discovered the pale, forlorn, almost lifeless figure of her abandoned teenage self. I said to her, knowing her identification with her father: 'Did your father ever have any severe pain, anything like this?' She said she did not think so, for although he died of heart trouble, being found dead in his study, she had never seen him in any pain that she remembered. But she considered it. She telephoned me some hours later saying that it did seem of help considering the two centres of pain—hers and the possible one of her father—and that she now remembered that, some months before her father died, there were indications that he was anticipating his death and had taken great care of himself. So in all probability he had had a heart attack before and thus, almost certainly, a bout of severe pain. We may note here that after her father's death the patient had a blackout with loss of memory, a period of sleep beyond the ordinary, from which she emerged a changed personality.

A few days after the telephone call I received a note which said: 'The recent discovery about one of the causes of the pain continues to have an amazing effect of peace, also the sense of having achieved something, the rest, after an almost too heavy task, the "Everest of the mind", which I of course could not have carried out alone.'

Here you see: linking back, feeding back the pain of the present moment to her place of critical hurt, to the pain of her father with which presumably she had identified herself, completed the circuit, so releasing the tension that was causing the present pain, the symptom or, one might say, the call coming up through the decades. You can feel from what she wrote what effort it took, but the 'Everest of the mind' she reached may well mean at the same time the peak of her own endeavour *and* the point where she could finally differentiate herself from the pain and fear of loss of her father who, one might say, is on the 'Everest', the 'rest for ever' of the mind — she could let him die.

In a severe, relatively uncomplicated case one can grasp what happens, but when a succession of rebuffs, each in themselves not of a critical nature, add up to the feeling of severe rejection, it is not so easy to locate and assess the critical damage. We will take a moment in the person's life when its growth is reaching out towards maturity. As the study of child development shows, there are a series of such buddings, such as from baby to toddler, from toddler to boyhood and on to adolescence, and similarly for girls, to what one might call the dawn of woman or man. It is at these special points in time and growth that their new experience of themselves — which, like all new things, at the moment of emergence is of a sensitiveness and vulnerability often difficult to comprehend for an adult — that these new developments of the personality, with their new imaginary and tentative experiments in life, need to be received with loving recognition and, if possible, conscious understanding of their nature. If these special moments of budding are not attended to and received with warmth, they are the proper points for critical hurt to occur. For here a division of the personality can take place which may leave it separated from its previous healthy growth. The undamaged early part is the portion that carries the colourful, individual and vital *joie de vivre*, the kind of person that most of us may have been fortunate enough to experience during the relaxation of holiday time and conviviality. You may have heard it said: 'He becomes human when he is a little drunk.' On the other hand, it is the compromised part that carries the burden of everyday living.

In cases of serious injury, the cut-off healthy pattern carries a critical amount of vital libido, the lack of which cripples or severely hampers the ongrowing personality. The young healthy part may reappear with a fairy-like quality. It comes and goes, like the family dog that vanishes for several hours if the house atmosphere is uncongenial, say, because of the tension of clashing personalities. Or, to bring it nearer home, like the independent young child that disappears into the attic or the bottom of the garden. It often, as it were, takes to the woods, and if that has been its necessary habitation and shelter for some time, to entice it back will take all the patience, ingenuity and understanding that it takes to lure a squirrel down from the tree. Indeed, in activating the imagery of that area, it is my experience that the psyche uses little animals and birds to manifest itself to the ego, on which they ultimately depend for their life here and now—the ego that has to carry on with the best compromise it can reach with its environment.

In order to bring a sense of healing that has real depth and a lasting quality, and returns to the injured one some of the zest of living of which he was so deprived, relationship has to be made with that healthy part of the stem of the personality beneath the damaged area that ever since had only been in sporadic contact with the struggling-on personality. If the analyst has an aware-ness of this vital position and is on the lookout for any manifesta-tion of it, this will most unexpectedly help and speed up the recovering process.

Eleanor

As an example of how the *feed-back*, the relating back of mature life experience to the area of original hurt, works out in practice, I take you to my consulting room again, so as to introduce you to Eleanor. She is a senior welfare officer of academic university standing, at the top of her profession, unmarried, in her middle forties. Much like 'Mrs. Somerset', she came to me in a state of despair; her life no longer had meaning, and her existence to her had no *raison d'être*, despite all the meaning of life she was bringing to others.

Eleanor had had a certain amount of psychotherapy in the past three or four years; originally she had come to it because she had become extremely involved in the course of her work with what one might call a border-line delinquent. It was one of those intelligent girls whom people are continually trying to help, whom every 'new broom' feels they can do something for, but who in the course of a few weeks or months fall back again into their pattern of delinquency. This young woman had begun to tyrannise over Eleanor to an amazing degree, calling her up on the telephone, borrowing money from her, and was trying to, and to a large extent had succeeded, in turning Eleanor into a bountiful, inexhaustible mother—an expectation of her which, despite her professional competence, she felt hard to resist.

The fundamental fact about Eleanor's pattern of life, like many others, was that since she could remember she had never felt it safe, secure or right to live out of her own self, but '*was* lived' under the *authority of what she felt was expected of her*.

To be in such a way 'lived' under the authority of an expectation I have found is one of the most crippling authorities for any human being to live under, because then you are counterfeiting yourself, you are living not your own pattern—which you have come through the millennia to reach—but out of a desperate need, to attain the minimum amount of security to survive, you have to shape yourself according to the expectations of the parental authority which you feel, and often it is only too true, will not accept you unless you conform to its pattern. It can be a very serious situation. One is dealing with something which was inaugurated with the intensity, and is lived under the insecurity, of a life-and-death situation.

Her real difficulty had started as early as at six months. Usually it comes up when the individual first had a sense of himself (or herself) as an individual, around four to six years old. Her earliest memory seemed to correspond to this time. This was of stamping her foot, aged five, and saying: 'I am not my sister, I am me.' Then a little later we found that something desperate, a catastrophe, had happened to the family when she was being nursed by her mother.

At aged six months, her brother, aged four and a half, the only son and the apple of the parents' eye, became ill with diphtheria and had to go to a fever hospital. Mother was nursing little Eleanor, so could not reach her only son, who died after a few weeks. From that time on there was a shadow over the family. The only son had died, the father felt that no longer was he working for his son and heir and, since he was a rather precarious personality, the light of his life went out and the reason for his work fell away. The father's ambition had been invested in this young boy, for whom he had hoped to build up a business, and it may give you some idea of the intensity of his feeling when I tell you that he started to call his young daughter *Bill*. This means that he was so under the image spell of the son who had died that he was unable to accept his little girl as a daughter—in fact, incapable of really acknowledging her existence. Your existence is not your own unless you are received as the person you are.

As to the relationship of the *mother* to her little daughter, we have seen that she was unable to reach her dying young son because she could not leave her baby daughter whom she was nursing, and besides that she would have had to go to a fever hospital. So we find a mother deprived of the last moments (and, possibly, with the phantasy of saving her son, of rescuing him) because of this newcomer to the family who was a girl—again not a boy.

Now, whereas we saw the father ignored his little daughter, the mother carried the love she had for the son over to her. However, out of fear that, if the daughter did anything out of herself, she would perish, the mother inhibited all spontaneous expression in the daughter. The fear of losing this new-born one tinged all her relationship to it.

This attitude was so persistent that Eleanor relates that her crucial, critical incident happened when at the age of six, she was out shopping with her mother. When not far from home, she had the sudden idea that she could get home all by herself. There was a busy street to cross, which she did with great care, looking left and right, and she arrived home—buoyant with this happy achievement. Mother found that her little girl had disappeared, thought of the street she had to cross, went, I believe, enquiring of the police; eventually she arrived home, found her daughter there, but her state was so frantic that Eleanor feared that she had almost killed her mother.

The mother had obviously gone through all the shattering fear, anguish and despair of again losing a child. So when finally she arrived home, she did not, could not, see the happiness of her little daughter in her great achievement of independent self-realisation, perhaps the first of that character in her life. She was so overwhelmed by the anticipated loss that she could not greet the living child joyfully or even properly; on the contrary, little Eleanor suffered one of her greatest shocks as the result of her independent action.

This was only one example in the child's life of experiencing that any spontaneous action endangered Mother's life. From then on she had to learn to control her natural self to such a degree that all spontaneity became impossible.

We are now in a position to see the kind of pattern that the parents wove out of this situation, the family relationship that resulted from the loss of their son and that the daughter found when she started to grow into life. She had in some way to adapt to it, if she was to survive.

Thus Eleanor is in the grip of, encaged by, both mother and father. If she behaves like a little girl and not like a boy, her father repudiates her; in fact, she heard her father say later: 'All women are stupid, stupid emotionally.'

Perhaps worse than that, if she reacted at all according to her nature, she threatened, and still feels to threaten, her mother's life, and thus, by killing her, to lose her own life.

Therefore, to her, *spontaneity* now brings the fear of death, and so does anything coming near her most critical hurt area, for it carries the terror, the death threat of the original situation, experienced at an age when she was still in 'participation mystique' with her mother.

As we can realise: to grasp, to keep related to these areas during analysis and to bring them towards healing is quite a task for both analysand and analyst.

From the first interviews and the assessment of the area of critical hurt onwards, I asked myself how could this be connected with her occupation as a psychiatric social worker, the devoted work with which she was almost destroying her life. I therefore suggested to her to be on the lookout in her work for those cases and individuals who specially caught her attention and in which she felt an emotional reaction — in other words, those situations that activated her unconscious.

While being attentive to such reactions, we also have to keep in mind the question why she chose the particular field of welfare work, that is, child guidance, to which she devoted her life and energies. In their basic training several lines are open to a psychiatric worker, such as work in mental hospitals, with delinquent mental defectives, and so on. The psychiatric social worker is concerned with both the child and the parent in the family situation. It is significant that Eleanor felt drawn to this sphere after trying others. Her intuition had scanned the whole field and selected the one where, unknowingly, she would be giving to others what she needed to give back to herself, as she finally discovered through this particular kind of analysis.

On my request to notice those cases which particularly caught her attention and so activated her unconscious, she soon brought relevant information. First she said she found herself specially concerned with children that had bad mothers.

We found that her *own* mother had, because of her anxiety, proved quite impossible for her to relate to naturally. She had given it up as hopeless and was even now as an adult just trying to keep her mother alive by sacrificing her own life to her, since she felt if she did not, then her mother's life would be endangered. That is, she was spending her weekends and holidays simply answering the demands of her mother, so that she had really no private life of her own. Her professional life gave her no personal fulfilment either.

As for the *father*, we saw that his ambition and *joie de vivre* were overshadowed by the death of his son and heir. He did not exert any active, only a negative influence; he withdrew behind deafness and had actually retired from business as soon as he could afford it. He was really little more than a part of the inner properties of the house.

Thus to Eleanor her mother was the predominant factor; she could not alter her. In her work, bad mothers attracted her, whom she found more accessible to her professional and scientific attention, and many of whom she was able to make better mothers for their children. In other words, she gave to these children what she could not give to herself—better mothers.

As we have seen before, what brought Eleanor first to analysis was her desperate involvement with a delinquent young girl whom she set out to save where others had been unable to do so. It is worth while looking into the part that this girl plays in Eleanor's life.

Quite in general, a delinquent child is a rebel who dares to assert his individuality over against the parental or collective authority. This, of course, often leads to nonsense, even destruction, because they lack the parental guidance or experience in their new enterprise. On the other hand, the delinquent in the family is often the hero figure, the one who is daring to attack, to break the vicious circle of maybe two or three generations.

Now we know that Eleanor, after heroic attempts up to age six, had found it impossible to go her own way, but she literally was in the situation of a rebel child, and although she had given it up, there was the hero girl still in her who in her depths had *not* given it up, that part of her which probably also enabled her to continue her analysis during a period of years when it took great courage and persistence. Because of maternal condemnation she had had to suppress the brave girl within her, and it became a negative shadow figure, a 'delinquent'. Now, in this girl whom she met in her work, she unconsciously met the delinquent hero in herself. But although seemingly so negative, that figure carried the high honour and burden of guarding a critical place in her lifeline. This accounts for the gruelling contest which outwardly went on with this intelligent and vital client. Inwardly from her side, all the resources she could bring to bear from her scientific and professional training, plus the activation of the unconscious, were brought into play. Here she would have had the opportunity to feed two sides of herself. On the one hand, she could see the positive qualities of that allegedly delinquent girl in herself, completely submerged in her depths, and on the other hand she could be the good mother. Yet as long as this happened unconsciously, it had a self-destroying effect. Here we see why this was a barren and sterile endeavour. She was pouring out herself, her time, money and nervous energy. Her life could no longer be called her own, night or day. She might have to respond to the demands of this shadow aspect, the heroic side of herself which seemed to have materialised in her patient. It was the unlived life of the little girl within who had had to give up the struggle, but whose undaunted spirit parted company in the shadow to await the time when it could be accepted, when there would be an ego strong, conscious and experienced enough to welcome it so as to come once again out into the flow of life.

Eleanor's actual life was one of hateful submission to a demand, devoted to preventing her mother from killing herself, as it were. The hero girl's part was essential in converting her life into one that was lived with a self-responsibility so that she could answer her own rightful calls for self-expression. Because this was acted out only professionally and not fed back to her own personal self, to *her* place of inner need, there was a barren, sterile, self-destroying aspect in the relationship to her work. However, as she engaged in it, as it were, right to the very limit of her resources, the relationship forced her to come to analysis, that is, to undertake the crucial task of bringing this courageous girl within her into consciousness.

From the very beginning the pattern of the original hurt is reflected in the symptoms and in the life pattern of the individual and may well repeat itself in the patient's relationship to the analyst. The image of the terrible father as well as that of the devouring mother, for instance, will at some time or other be transferred to the analyst and acted out, and likewise of the loving one; that is a straightforward example. But the pattern can be very subtle, and so it is worth while suggesting that the awareness of this *pattern* should be kept in mind throughout the analysis, especially in times of difficulty which during its course are bound to arise.

An example of this occurred to me with Eleanor. She had grasped the importance to her of her own hero girl, and that in turn released her relationship to the delinquent girl. Her analytical work was good and developing well. Her area of original hurt had been traced and surveyed. In addition to her courageous self, several helpful, cut-off and inadequately related-to parts of her personality had become personified and, to some extent, had been brought back, fed back, into her life. But then, to my distress, things became stuck. At least, it was a sticky patch; there seemed to be what one might call vague resistances despite good will. So together we went into the difficulty.

We came to where resistances against the spontaneous and trusting and wholehearted analytical work had almost brought her progress to an end. I found that *I* had become the carrier of the most negative strand in her area of critical hurt. That was, wherever she felt to be needed, she had to find out and do what was expected of her. We discovered that she had been working with the idea that I expected her to produce what she did.

Although she really produced what was appropriate and rightful, yet it was, as it were, done under the wrong authority and not out of the spontaneous creativeness so necessary for development during analysis. I might add here that, in looking into my own inwardness as one very much needs to in these happenings, I found that there might have been a grain of truth; of course, I was not to that extent expecting things, but because the development accorded very much with my own thesis, it is quite likely that, being human, my attitude had been tinged with expectation.

This taught me a great lesson. When a person is endeavouring to do what is expected of him or her, especially when the expecting person is invested with some authority, then the ego is on guard, suspicious, not wholehearted but divided. Such patients are in a precarious state to a greater or lesser degree. There is doubt 'whose lifeline are they serving'. It is self-evident that, in this state, sound growth cannot take place.

As has been said, I had steadily drawn Eleanor's attention to be on the lookout for all occasions on which her unconscious was activated by incidents or people in her work. One day she arrived with more than her usual eagerness and the wish to express herself. She had, she said, found in her work an example of what might be called a *ghost father*. A young girl of eight had been brought to the clinic by her mother for stealing. The girl was in a greatly disturbed state. Four years before, the father had been killed in the war. There was more to it, however, than even the impact on the child of the loss of her father when she was four. The mother was a keen spiritualist and, although the father was dead, she was keeping him alive in an uncanny way. She was so to speak

in daily contact with him so that, to the child, the father was dead
yet was also alive. The child's nature, battling gallantly with the
situation, as all healthy children do, was unable to make anything
of this father who was both dead and alive, and consequently the
girl was greatly puzzled and disturbed. Feeling deprived of natural
attention, she had begun to steal. Now, to my patient, Eleanor,
this situation brought a discovery of the first order: 'That was
what happened to me!' she exclaimed. 'My brother really died
when I was six months, yet in some queer way he was eternally alive
ever in the house.' With this insight, her relationship to *this ghost
of her brother* became more positive and constructive. Through the
girl in the clinic she could not only observe intellectually but feel
with a wave of emotional response what had happened to herself
and build up a healthy direct relationship with her own inner
brother image. She could now attend to her own inner needs more
successfully. Previously both her inner and outer contacts had
been unhealthy, queer, a mixture of relationship and estrangement.

Here then is a telling example of how the idea of the feed-back
works out in practice. Eleanor had found in her professional field a
pattern that mirrored almost directly one in her own area of critical
hurt, as the delinquent girl had done before. However, whereas before she had not been aware of the link between outside reality and
her own inner need and had, therefore, with distressing consequences, tried to deal with it outwardly, this time it was different.
The insight she required for her clinical case was that which she
needed for herself. Because of the knowledge developed in her analysis, she was able to relate it to the corresponding place within her.
She quickly felt and consciously realised the correspondence between the ghost father in the outer reality of her vocational field and
the ghost brother in that of her own critical hurt. Neither had been
allowed to take up their natural position in the psyche. But now
the circuit was completed. Her vocational field became directly
related to that of critical hurt, and along this return arc of the
circuit the appropriate experiences were fed back. Thereby she
became healthily connected with that very important part of herself, the family ghost brother. This flash completed, as it were,
the return arc and thus released into consciousness the energy
dormant in that complex. Distressing as had been her experience
with the delinquent girl, that of her ghost brother could be, and
indeed was, healing, because this figure was brought out from the
shadow, became positive after having been negative and, above all,
could now be included in her life instead of being cut off in
isolation.

Since then she was much steadier and much surer in her attitude to her inner self. Henceforth, she was able to relate more naturally to her inner figures, more directly and thus also free of the expectations which previously she had projected on to me. Consequently, her relationship to me also became easier, so that as it were I could become more of a positive father, one that allows her to have her own experience. It seems that this spontaneous experience of hers which, as she felt, arose quite independently of her analysis, yielded a standpoint which gave her a more healing contact with me and her analytical work.

We recall how negatively she had been related to her delinquent patient and that she had been trying to work out, to get through to, to heal her inner separation and estrangement through an abortive, exhausting and destroying attempt to help someone *outside* herself. Now, in her new connection within the analytical situation, she was, one might say, still battling but in a positive, enriching way.

An interesting detail will highlight the change. The borderline girl was heaping up telephone calls by getting them reversed, to be paid for by Eleanor who had accepted them for quite some time. Now, after this inner recovery of the archetypal, rightful relationship to her brother image, Eleanor herself was using telephone calls, but much less expensive ones, to ring *me* up several times a week while she was ill with flu, just merely to ascertain that I was still there and available.

This may sound a very strange position to put oneself in, but I have found that in these newly-won personalities, when they are just establishing themselves, a special continuity of relationship is often absolutely necessary, and it is not really an extravagant use of my own time, because painfully and by error, I have discovered that if I do not give them that appropriate time and opportunity, the work may be put back by months, whereas it will be maintained by understanding acceptance, say, of such telephone calls — as long as they remain within acceptable limits. But in these cases, which really have a life-and-death quality, I have never found them misused.

Basil

In the following example we will turn to an acute traumatic experience of childhood where, as in many such cases, the effects of the injury are carried upward throughout the subsequent phases of development. We find the adult with both a distorted and damaged picture of himself which has a double-sided effect on his relationships with his environment: (1) he projects his negative feelings and (2) he tends to manipulate his relationships so as to confirm the distorted picture which he has of himself, and so becomes more and more convinced of his unhappy self-assessment.

Negative as this is, it also provides an opportunity during analysis to reach and to heal the original situation. It is almost as if, again and again, in the hope of being recognised and eventually dealt with by an understanding adult, the original trauma were repeated so that it can be redeemed after all those years.

One can even find such a damaging pattern being carried on to the third and fourth generation, until finally some individual is able to find release and start a dynasty that is purged of it.

In the present case, the pattern was that of a man of forty-five years whom we will call Basil. He was sent to me after the sudden death of his last analyst, the two previous ones having also died during his analytical work with them.

His problems were: (*a*) feeling of inferiority; (*b*) self-depreciation; (*c*) the murderer within him; as he put it: 'My problem is a fear, when an impulse comes over me I have to go against all reason, when it is there it is almost overwhelming'; (*d*) he had difficulties in getting on with his colleagues, up to the point of losing his job; (*e*) lastly, he was partially impotent with his wife.

His difficulties, as he remembered them, started at three and a half years, when his father first deserted his mother and, shortly afterwards, his mother left him, the boy, to follow another man to a distant part of the world. He was left in charge of a sadistic grandmother who on occasions beat him unmercifully. In his own words: 'I felt this feeling of longing for mother would kill me. All I needed was to be with Mummy again. One day, walking down the second flight of stairs in the house, I felt mother's black shadow in the distance who would not allow me near her. I realised there was no hope, nothing could release this enormous pain within me.' Asked what happened to 'this longing that would kill you', he said: 'it went into blackness and nightmares'.

His mother having left him, his grandmother being inaccessible, he finally tried the servants to comfort him in his nightmares. But unfortunately, as he told me, they, being outcasts themselves in that part of the world, would not take friendly to a deserted small boy. And although he continued to sleep in their quarters, his sense of rejection was increased rather than helped.

I was able to see two photographs of his childhood: one at about four years, showing an intelligent, relaxed little boy, though with anxious eyes; the other, of about eight years with his grandmother and mother, who had temporarily returned, a physically drawing back, unhappy figure. He commented: 'Here you see the scringer that is in me' whereas, to me, it was the photo of a desolate resisting boy rather than that of a coward which Basil had implied. The first photo was that of a relatively undamaged child, the other being in the grip of the traumatic situation.

Looking back on this period during our sessions, he said to me: 'If I had been attractive, then grandmother would have liked me and mother would not have left me.' This feeling of being unworthy of love was so ingrained in him that even the fact that in his professional work with handicapped children he was outstandingly competent and successful, especially in restoring self-esteem to badly damaged boys, had not altered this depreciating relationship to himself.

In describing these circumstances, it became quite clear that he still clung to his old, almost perverse idea of himself, although many of his experiences could have helped him to correct it.

Two to three years later, when his mother reappeared out of nowhere, no contact was established. Even worse, he recalled a scene that when he asked his mother for permission to do something, she answered: 'Ask grandmother.' He replied: 'Grandmother is not my mother—you are.' 'And I realised', he added, 'that Mother was not very much on my side.'

Soon after this scene he started to refuse to have anything to do with grown-ups, was readily disobedient, kicked and screamed and had many beatings. So by this time his feeling of himself, of his value, dignity and worthwhileness had been so damaged that it became overlaid with a symptomatic reaction pattern, of regressing to the earlier times when his mother was still with him: he started to wet and soil his bed and, as he put it, 'became a messy, unlikeable little brat like a diseased animal, wetted and messed. Something snaps—you think you are doing the right thing, but it is the wrong.'

When he was nine years old, his father suddenly appeared on the scene, brought him to England for schooling and duly vanished again. Although he had been at school before, yet at that age he could not read or write. At his prep school, he said, he was repeatedly beaten for being a coward at football for not tackling; nevertheless, he was in the first team. As to his intellect, he noted: 'Difficult to work—only phantasy. Like lying in a morass and not being able to lift an arm. A slough of despondency, oppressed by failure.' Yet another time he said: 'At prep school I was "cocky", too bright, too quick; if excited, eager, I went pale.'

9

It was not before the age of thirteen, according to his memory, that he had the experience of someone showing him some ordinary loving affection: it was in England when he was staying for the holidays with a nice married couple.

Following the prep school he went to public school. He was as unhappy there as he had been elsewhere.

When he was seventeen years, he managed to get permission to leave school and for a year he became an unpaid cowman on a farm. This, he said, was the happiest year of his life. Then his father turned up and took him back to his country, saying in reply to his protest: 'I want to get some of my money back which I've spent on you.' The war brought him back to Europe; he got a commission and spent several years in Africa.

Listening to his life story, with an occasional question or comment, I looked for opportunities to point out his negative perspective of his experience, be it an achievement or, occasionally, an apparent failure. However much one speaks the truth as one sees it, the decisive factor is that in analysis the patient himself comes to judge these events with as similar an objectivity as he would view one of the difficult boys under his care.

I rather anxiously and apprehensively explored his war record. I was quite prepared to hear that he had damaged his career by some outburst with his fellow officers and the authorities. But, on the contrary, he had served with credit, achieving on one occasion a most difficult movement of men and lorries through what was thought to be an impossible terrain in Central Africa—in one place, he said, for fifteen miles the wheels of the lorries never touched the ground but went from boulder top to boulder top.

Further he confessed that, when he was finally leaving Africa because of ill health, he received a message from a staff officer to come and see him, an officer he did not like and took for granted did not like him either. They had a drink together, and to his surprise this man told him that 'at first we thought very little of you, but now I would like to let you know that we feel quite differently and have greatly admired what you have done'; with that the 'interview' ended.

I have learned that, for many of us, a confession of achievement can be of greater significance than the better known confessions of sins, and it may often be as hard or even harder to create the right atmosphere for it. From this repeated experience I have come to the conclusion that it is an offence, nay a sin, not to acknowledge to oneself, as freely and fully as one is able to, what one has achieved.

Part of my work is to help the damaged to develop this often very difficult attitude to themselves. Their personal depreciation is supported by a collective notion. The Victorian Christian up-bringing was to stress our sins and to diminish our achievements, out of a misguided feeling that self-depreciation may protect us from so-called spiritual pride that would lead us into a damaging presumptuousness. But for each of us it is as if each growing phase is a child, our offspring, that has a need for, and a right to, an acknowledgment of its achievements. All growing things have this need—what child can grow in health without it? A young thing is so insecure.

To return to Basil, he had developed a gastric ulcer and found himself in a strange way a Yoga type of healer who cured him in three months. Whatever the methods of this, as it turned out later, unbalanced man, he gave to Basil the first experience of a loving and caring father he ever had; the healing effect of this affection is also of special interest from a psychosomatic point of view. As he put it: 'He was like an adopted father—kindness personified. But he had an untruthful optimism, so I could not stay with him.'

We repeatedly went through his life story, looking out for damage at the important phases as well as of rightful self-confidence and undoubtedness. I could help him to spot the bully in himself, to hold and see with some compassion those occasions when he did not come up to his high ideals of manhood and, above all, to give attention to the present-day events in his per-sonal and professional life which, however small in themselves, reflect both the old reactive pattern and the freeing from it, the new achievement. These so-called minor occasions are so impor-tant because they carry an intensity which is not too great for him to handle and learn from.

After Basil had returned to his home country, at first as a cowboy on a ranch, he became assistant manager on a large coffee estate. He evidently handled the workers well and competently but readily developed antagonistic relationships with his colleagues and superiors. When he finally left, his tough, unpopular chief said to him: 'Well, anyhow you are the only one whom I knew would be telling me the truth and not kowtow to me like the others.' ('I would not knuckle down to him, I had a strong feeling of integrity. I had integrity.')

After this last unsuccessful attempt to settle down in his home country, feeling that what to him was a superficial life almost amounting to suicide, he finally returned to England. Here he took what he called in his self-depreciation a low-pass degree in psychology. From there he went into teaching. When he came to me he was a teacher for so-called backward children. He told me that a large proportion of them were backward because of emotional blockage, not because of low intelligence.

What made me feel at the first interview that this damaged man was of a special quality and in a positive though unconscious relationship to healing, was his statement that several epileptic boys in his group ceased to have fits after they had been with him for some time and others who had specialised in stealing ceased to do so, though one relapsed when he himself had to be away from school for a period.

Basil is a remarkable example of a deeply damaged personality with an almost catastrophic trauma at three and a half, being led by some strange caring instinct to a field of activity where he could give to others, to emotionally damaged boys, that caring understanding which he himself would have so needed at similar phases of life. Having in his professional work a whole field of experience where he had to deal with these and related handicaps, he discovered his ability to bring these boys back nearer to their potential health, to what I would call their entelechy. In our sessional encounters I was on the alert when his expressions seemed to be spontaneous and to come from his centre. I collected 'key phrases' such as when on many occasions he was calling himself a coward, yet on others he quite unexpectedly would bring something out, with a lightness of touch and spontaneity, with a naivety as would the undisturbed one within him, who I then knew had survived. It is like reconstructing a very damaged mosaic; islands may come up or areas still be recognisable in their original freshness. From these areas one may attempt to, and often to a large degree achieve, a realisation of what the artist, the creator, meant it to be.

By using every opportunity, however small, as long as it has the right resonance, I try to bring about a restoration of the distorted and damaged image the patient carries of himself. As to the little boy of four to five years who had repeatedly to give in to the murderous assaults of his grandmother and was left with the feeling of humiliation, I would point out that this was for sheer survival's sake. Subsequently, whenever an occasion activated that area, he had called himself a coward and, when deeply enough hit, felt so blacked out that he was immobilised or else he got raised to a state of intense aggression, quite out of proportion to the actual situation.

We might say if this man had a constitutional tendency to

epilepsy, he would most certainly have had epileptical fits on some of these occasions. In his own words: 'I felt like a blanket being pulled over my head. I lost power of judgment and became incoherent.' In other words, specifically patterned energy becomes undifferentiated and takes charge of the total person. For the duration of one of these states the individual as such is annihilated.

In moments of rising aggression, however, his fear was that 'the murderer within him might act out'. In discussing occasions when he had experienced one or the other aspect of this syndrome, we re-enacted it together in a constructive way. He would revive the details of the situation, the vividness of which I would at the same time support by strengthening his feeling that it was safe here and now to let fly. Whilst, however, personifying and acting out the young boy in him at that moment, and thus also relating to him, he would try to discover and understand what brought about such rage.

And then I would draw on his adultness in his professional field, on his repeated successful experiences in dealing with such desperate acting out in children and recalling to his conscious awareness how he handled them, with subtlety, compassionate but firm understanding and great patience. Thus we would finally reach the stage of what I call the feed-back, using his own experience with so-called maladjusted children, his true vocational field. There he had learned—as I would put it in my words—that delinquency with which we are faced in a present situation, has so often originally been a healthy and intelligent reaction to a life-threatening experience. By helping him to apply this comprehensive insight to his own boyhood syndrome and persistent pattern of reaction, he was challenged to feed it back to his own places of desperate need.

In this way, I could deal with his fear of violence, his feeling of inferiority; the so-called 'coward' became recognised as carrying a sadistic and inappropriate name for a child faced with actually paralysing powers. Eventually he could accept that, if he had persisted in standing up against overwhelming forces, he would have been irretrievably destroyed, and that it was the centre of his self-preservation that blacked him out till it was safe to emerge, decades later, in a tested and trustworthy environment.

Strangely, this feed-back is unbelievably resisted by the ill one because, in order to reach that depth and place of original hurt, he unavoidably has to experience the awfulness which originally caused the suspension of his vital values and thus his present desperation for which he came to seek help.

It is by the rediscovery of these basic values, overlaid, distorted and often repressed with the same destructive attitude
which at the time caused them to go out of circulation with the total
personality, that gradually the individual gets a truer image of who
he really is and of the powers that are available within him and are
on his side.

The last of his complaints for which he came to analysis was
what he had called his impotence. This was a theme he frequently
brought up and used in situations and for feelings other than sexual
ones. It seemed to be basically connected with his sense of utter
impotence in the face of the attacks of his grandmother. With this
helplessness we are right back in the traumatic situation of the
four-year-old. One day he had wandered some distance from his
house, which he was forbidden to do. He met a little girl who was
bathing in a stream and invited him to join her. Although too shy
to follow her invitation, he felt a deep urge to do so. When he got
back, he received from his grandmother a murderous beating with
a stick. This, by the way, came up as an association with a painting
he brought to a session, and he commented on another occasion:
'My grandmother must have been beating her own fear of sex out
of me . . . her own passion must have been enormously strong to
beat it down, to beat me so sadistically.'

It seems that, from this early experience and many similar ones,
his feeling of helplessness in the face of what he was then quite
naturally unable to cope with, became intermingled with many
others of a similar feeling tone. For example, on two occasions, one
at eleven and one at twelve years when he was taunted by another
boy, he was paralysed in action although, ordinarily, he would
have been quite capable of holding his own and mastering the
situation. When he recorded these experiences, he was so deeply
overcome with the shame of his impotence in the situation and it
was so out of character with his recollections of other comparable
occasions that the inhibiting factor must have been due to a crucial
interference with his very own basic nature. Linking this up with
the grandmother experience at four, it was possible to bring some
alleviation to this place of desperate humiliation.

Moreover, a fear of women was unavoidably interwoven in his
make-up. As I said, up to thirteen years his only relationship with
women had been with vicious ones. This is accentuated by his
own fear that he might destroy them during intercourse. And,
again, we could trace these fears to his natural wish to hit back
at his mother and tear her apart, as she had abandoned him.

To continue his story, he married in his own country when he came back from the war and had one daughter to whom he is deeply attached. The marriage was dissolved after thirteen years when his wife deserted him, going home to her own country under the pressure of her relatives. Here again the original trauma, to be left by his mother, was reactivated.

However, he married again two years before he consulted me, a colleague fifteen years younger than he. Once more there were quite some tensions in his marriage, but we found that when he stood up to his wife in a disagreement, which ordinarily filled him with fear and apprehension, the relationship improved, and with it his potency. As he could see, his impotence arose not from constitutional sexual defect but in any situation which activated the original feeling of helplessness.

Linking up with these and many other associated occasions gradually restored the feeling of his natural healthy self, so that the distortions of the powerful and dynamic shadows of his childhood are now lessening and the healthy image of himself which is his birthright begins to shine through again.

To sum up: the psychological idea of the *feed-back* is, after first tracing it, to return to the buried, early injured part, often indicated by that the *adult* personality is giving to others but cannot relate to by himself. The patient needs skilled analytical assistance to approach his inner wound because it is unbearable or even lethal, and thus blacked out or at least deep in the shadow.

Such work of feeding back has, furthermore, to be complemented by helping the conscious ego to link up again with the healthy earlier part of the personality cut off by the injury so that, eventually, regrowth can take place, as will be exemplified in the following pages. Only these two processes, together and maintained over a considerable period of time, will bring about a deep and secure sense of healing.

Time and again I have found that healing cannot be effective merely by the re-experiencing of the trauma itself. I believe that it is an important and necessary extension of the theory and practice of psychological healing, of analysis, to *combine* both these ideas of a *feed-back to the damaged area and of linking up the present adult personality with the healthy pre-injured part*. This may in many cases also lead to a considerable shortening of the treatment.

THE PROCESS OF REGROWTH

How then can healing in depth be brought about? What we have to try is to contact the human being at his period of critical hurt and shock. For, at that period, the personality became so to speak divided within itself: the one that lived on in the outer world carries with him the shock, the fear of that fateful experience, whereas the younger part detached itself and remained suspended, protected in the shadow area. This suspended unit has the healthy naivety, zest, vitality, sense of wonder and much more that is necessary for life. When it does come out, it will often be with the voice, the vocabulary and the imagery of that age. These inner figures may emerge from dreams, phantasies, etc. in human form as a child, a beloved person, etc. They may, however, also be activated by an actual child without, and surprisingly enough it may not even be a child but can be another adult whose unknown inner child may call out your own. Lastly, these figures may at first present themselves in the shape of what at that time held the greatest value—the cat, the dog, the teddy bear, and so on.

Basic conditions for them to emerge, however, are that the therapist, more even than we usually have to in deep analysis, has proved a trustworthy person and a safe place to relate to and that he can hold the apprehension, the guilt and the hurt which will assail these patients whenever an experience in the here and now activates the old wound and situation. First supported by the analyst, they are then gradually transferred, 'weaned back' to the care and attention of the adult patient. A continuous, compassionate though detached and highly responsible relationship to these inner figures has to be achieved. This is a synthesis which differs decisively from so-called reductive analysis, although including it.

I should like to add that, in describing the shut-off, cocooned part of the personality, I took care not to use the term 'split-off', in order to avoid the suggestion of schizophrenia.

It is to this submerged part of one's own being to which healing needs to be directed. A most sensitive and painstaking awareness, a specially tuned consciousness, are called for. Only something comparable to the most loving and understanding parental care can restore its confidence. And this has to be done over and over again —often in all sorts of circumstances, till the hurt one can co-operate. He will test you time and again before he will dare to relate, to come out of his retreat and with your help join once again with the mainstream of life.

Besides a deep yearning and a sense of urgent necessity for greater wholeness, willing to do all they can to achieve a fuller life, adult patients in particular need to be of strong fibre, with an ego of courage and integrity while working under their handicap, and co-operative in relating both to the analyst and to their own inner figures as they emerge. For they have to learn to hold their adult consciousness under the impelling fascination and the often disintegrating impact of these highly charged submerged units.

To illustrate a significant part of what I call healing in depth, I would like to take you with me to actual situations in which the recovery of a lost portion of the personality took place.

'Round the bend'

The first of these was with a highly trained and competent professional woman; she was efficient, conscientious and sensitive but complaining of a sense of hardening of her feeling, with some relevant psychosomatic symptoms and a strong undercurrent of suicidal tendencies.

The first years of her analysis meant intense sometimes hair-raising work. To give an example from the time when the transference was firmly established and I carried the father image: at my Harley Street consulting room the patients came up by lift and went down by stairs. At the end of one of the earlier interviews I had seen her off at the door leading downstairs which clicked slightly as I closed it; she had been the last patient of the day. Several minutes later a very shaken and frightened little woman crept up the stairs, back again to my rooms. The click of the door activated an overwhelming fear, obviously reaching back to an early traumatic experience: any separation tended to flood her with a passionate despairing emotion. Eventually we traced it back to the death, i.e. complete disappearance, of her father when she was eight, though there had been many separations from him before; he was a sailor and she had been father's little girl. About six months later I carefully tried out this click again, and it still promoted the terror reaction. It needed a long time to bring and knit together the injured parts, so that she could stand the parting moment.

At other times she got so close to areas of deep shock that a hot drink or a mild sedative was necessary, with an hour's waiting before it was safe to let her go home, and the goodbye arrangements involved a great deal of time and careful managing. Even then she might reappear after a quarter of an hour or so in a frightened state or, at other times, phone up once or twice on her way home, as if to make sure that I, the analyst, the person most important to her, was still there and alive. I found that her having one or two toffees to suck on the way back eased things quite a lot.

All these exhausting needs I hesitated and resisted to answer until I saw that the situation absolutely demanded it.

An almost shattering difficulty was when her only brother committed suicide. He was a clergyman of high quality and integrity who had tried to reach alone what I would call the place of critical hurt and heal it with insufficient help. His attempt ended in disaster because he did not realise the serious tensions involved in his endeavour, though one may wonder whether this might not have been his moment to die, and therefore beyond any human being's capacity to alter it. His loss, however, nearly torpedoed his sister's analysis. It needed a combined effort and the outer support of a good nursing home to come through the crisis.

This patient taught me that one cannot hurry them along. I had to let her proceed at her own pace, however exasperatingly slow it seemed to me at times, though checking constantly if I could not give her a lead that would help her forward and speed up the process. But almost as regularly this would be received by the phrase: 'That is too old' (i.e. too fast, too grown up).

In fact, she had to go through the experience of meeting, recognising and assimilating four or five young parts of herself, each with its own name, representing damaging experiences earlier in her life; every time it was quite an undertaking. I may illustrate this from a letter of hers which gives an impression of the reality of these inner children and the care they need: '. . . after a bad night I feel deflated and poorly, just like Hucky and Ben did. I have promised them to take it easy today and just to go into the garden a bit. With my eyes closed, I saw Hucky dancing about at the idea of going into the garden. I said "thank God" because, when I got up this morning, I thought they had gone and wouldn't come back any more. All because I have been going non-stop in the wrong atmosphere for a fortnight. I said: "I know you are poorly, and I have made you so. I am *very* sorry." I think it will be all right now.'

One of the memories which came up in the early part of her analysis was of herself at sixteen saying goodbye to her boy friend who was going away to the war. She had a vivid and most distressing picture of herself as a girl standing on the platform and watching the train disappear round the bend. This image came up repeatedly during the analysis, sometimes several months apart, always with a tremendous sense of overwhelming despair and hopelessness.

Of this adolescent girl within her she wrote in her notes: 'I can feel the loneliness of her, the shell-like nothingness. I could not talk to her, it was like talking to nothing; she felt like nothing, she stood empty, her heavy dark eyes looking into space.' A few days later: 'She is lolling on me, hanging round my neck.' A week later: 'Now there is this girl and *me*; she is herself and the young ones. Now she is hurting the young ones. I must not let her, I must help the young ones. She is doing it because *she* was hurt, *her* young part was hurt.'

Following an analytical session some time later, she sent me a letter: 'In the station on my way home I thought of suicide. I said: "I didn't get anything *there* (my consulting room) to make me feel better," but I sat with my eyes closed and hugged the awful feeling to myself. Later I said: "I have to be willing to feel how she felt." At home, after tea, I lay down. I burst into tears because I *was* her under the bedclothes. I began to think of everyday things. Cutting across my thoughts came "Darling!" That night when I went to bed, your voice said "warmth and comfort".' I may add here that, in answer to a telephone call when she was in despair, I did not know what to say, how to relate to this sad isolated being, and in my impasse, the words had come to me: 'Give her warmth and comfort.'

One Sunday afternoon I had a telephone call. She said, this 'picture' came back to her that afternoon; she had seen this girl waiting and watching the train disappear round the bend. This time she felt *she was* that girl, but at the same time she was *with* that girl, and she put her arm around her and held her closely and warmly, thus taking away the feeling of being lost and alone.

Now here something quite new had happened: the adult person had gone back within herself, had found this young girl within herself and had given her the recognition, the sympathy and understanding for which she herself had been waiting all along. Throughout these decades, she had unconsciously been trying to get a corresponding satisfaction from outside, yet no outer achievement could compensate for the lack of this basic inner relationship. So this young girl would have remained there for evermore, as a frozen part of herself, if the older part had not during her analytical work gained the experience to relate to this inner figure and found the compassion to go back and, finally, *herself* fetch her into the warm life of the here and now.

I myself was the parental, the significant mediating figure. To my astonishment this patient, always a most considerate woman, felt it urgently necessary to ring me up on a Sunday afternoon to tell me her news and share it. It was important to receive this message with an appropriateness that many errors, as well as successes, have taught me. For example, I have more than once answered the telephone or received her when she arrived with a greeting that was right for the professional *adult* person she is, and this upset to a serious degree an aspect of her younger personality who was the one waiting there eager to greet me and expecting a response in tune with that age.

The experience of the waiting girl seeing the train disappear round the bend, and many others like it, have helped me to understand how certain parts of the personality, imprisoned, locked up lower down in its stem, can be set free and recovered. Here I had the opportunity to participate in such a vital event.

We may ask what the effect of assimilating these entities to full consciousness has been on the patient. It has brought to her—and we remember that she had been suicidal—a sense of inner purpose and meaning in her life. Moreover, the relationship with her own inner resources has made her increasingly more independent both of me as her analyst and of outer circumstances. Instead of needing to be in almost continual touch with me, I now see her only at intervals of one or two months. This is what I mean by healing in depth.

The engineer

Next I want to convey some of the deep-reaching work with Duncan, an engineer, a sensitive man of strong fibre and high intelligence, in his mid-thirties when he came for analysis, now an executive in a large, international concern. He has two brothers, one older, one younger, no sisters; both parents were alive when he came, since then his father died.

Duncan came first to seek my help both from dissatisfaction over his sexual relationships which, though quite normal, lacked the sense of fulfilment, and because of difficulties in settling down to his work. In exploring the situation, I understood that he could not do a detailed project which was part of a larger whole, because in order to get down to detail, he had to grasp the total and its significance beforehand. He was, I found, so deeply divided in himself that, in order to balance it, he needed wholeness, the totality of comprehension, to a fantastic degree. He was as sensitive to any lack of balance in a situation as a highly musical ear is to a tune slightly off-key or a pilot to a small list of his plane or ship, and any deviation would affect him to the point of anguish and desperation.

Feeling awful despite everything seemingly being right also interfered in his relationship with the other sex. Because of his unconscious sensitivity for wholeness which he could not achieve, any affair with a girl gave an aftermath of deep dissatisfaction and even despair, up to his late twenties.

When on a mission to America he had fallen in love, he was completely mobilised by the experience, but the girl, who mirrored in some way his mother, was unaffected and asked him: 'What's come over you? Why can't you behave like other guys?' There was a hangover from this for a long time.

Then he met another, 'more human' girl, as he put it. He was not impotent but could not relate to her with his feeling.

His analysis was rather unusual. It did not grip him at first. He had come chiefly for practical reasons of his work, and I could give some help with this immediate problem. Only after his return from the U.S.A. did the analysis slowly begin to take hold. He suffered from a state of anxiety, was ill at ease, out of balance with himself. Being subject to moods seriously interfered with his self-expression and activities. Correspondingly, instead of friendly, co-operative relations he had either unfriendly or too friendly, undifferentiated ones.

We can find the basis of his difficulties in his relationship to his parents. They were of incompatible temperament, his mother a passionate, wildly intuitive type, chaotic in both her emotional and domestic life, the father a steady, rational Scottish business-man who desperately tried to maintain a sense of order and sanity in the house. With all his mother's warmheartedness and affection, the boy had to go to school with torn and inappropriate clothing, although there was no material reason for it, and the household was in such a mess that the boys could never ask friends in.

The contrast between his parents, his mother who, affectionate but moody and unreliable, was totally unable to think clearly, and his father, entrenched in his practical Scottish clearmindedness but equally unable to trust feeling, explains why a man of Duncan's intellectual capacity could, as he was, be afraid of thinking. He possibly mistrusted it because he had experienced in his parents' unhappy marriage that his father's rationalistic approach could not balance his mother's disturbed feeling or reach her heart. Correspondingly, he was hampered by being divorced from feeling, as his father was, and from thinking as his mother was. To other people, however, he appeared as a good mixer, and few would guess his inner distress.

It will not be surprising that this resulted in a crippling of his personality. In order to go forward at all, he had to suppress, cut himself off from, either his feeling or his thinking — so much so that, on one occasion, he dreamt that he greeted a man and instead of extending an ordinary arm, he tendered a hook arm which was his.

With his innate sensitiveness this, I believe, may account for the desperate anguish he experienced at times, and the deep sense of need which kept him to and carried him though analysis. The hook arm in the dream seems to symbolise a mechanical substitute for a natural human relationship. On the other hand, what may have helped him to maintain his sanity and to survive, was his choice of engineering which allowed his sensation and intuition to take the lead and thinking and feeling coming in, as it were, unobserved by the side.

Duncan tended seriously to undervalue his achievements, being unable to differentiate between how they were outwardly received and their actual value, to assess them in their own right. Such a degree of damage to the feeling of self-valuation is one of the deepest and severest causes of later illness. It usually originates in the early achievements of the ego, as it was first establishing itself, not being recognised and valued as what they were really worth at that age. For instance, his first walking steps were met with the remark: 'Oh yes, but you staggered like a top-heavy boy.' Another comment, when at the age of four he was proudly painting a house, was: 'That's not a house, that's an old box.' Such a reception of the opening bud of feeling of achievement lies at the basis of a serious self-depreciation of the ego, as I have repeatedly experienced in patients.

To show you how such early damage is carried on in adult life and will even constellate non-recognition of brilliant achievements, let me tell you the following story. As a junior captain during the last war, Duncan had to take a flying-boat and its crew from England to Africa. Taxiing through the waters of the home harbour, the huge plane was caught in an unusual pattern of cross-currents and waves which caused it to behave in an unmanageable way. He applied correctly all the techniques he had been taught for correcting a ship under such conditions, but without effect. The boat was in imminent danger of disaster. He decided that the only thing to do was to open the throttle and go ahead at full speed. This corrected the instability to a large extent, but presently the harbour boom, closing the harbour against submarines, loomed up ahead, threatening a crash. Duncan had to make a quick and awesome decision, to try and lift the boat over the boom, a unique undertaking in his experience and probably

for pilots much more senior than he. With masterly skill he succeeded in doing it, except for some slight damage to a few rear
plates of the hull, the repair of which caused his flight a delay of
several days. He was so upset by this minor damage to the ship
and the delay that, totally unaware of himself and his achievement,
his report gave no indication of his presence of mind, wit and skill
in preventing complete disaster. Instead of being commended for
an outstanding performance, he just got away with it as something
that could not be helped, that is, he narrowly escaped being
reprimanded. When he came to see me, his morale was still overwhelmed by this event, and for months I had to use every suitable
occasion to relate him to it, until at last he was able to honour
himself more or less rightfully for it.

As a young man he had joined, for a short time, the Communist
Party, as he remembered only in the later part of his analysis—he
would have linked up with any party that would annihilate,
liquidate, abolish that pattern of society which would not, could
not, recognise him, which as he felt had no place for him with his
values.

Duncan's basic conflict, however, had occurred in his growing
period right through the main years of ego formation. Time and
again he found that his mother wanted him habitually to be there
for her sake, not his, that he was not really felt, considered or even
listened to by her as himself—as he put it: 'Mother never saw me
as me.' This, I think, explains his self-depreciation, his dependence
on outside acknowledgment and, last but not least, his longing for a
total relationship and his despair in being unable to achieve it.

The conflict consisted, on the one hand, in his trying to give to
his mother all that her husband could not and, on the other hand,
the natural instinctual trends of a young boy and adolescent, say
from six to sixteen, whose urge to life was not yet entirely suspended to a damaging extent. Instead of being allowed to follow
his own interests and purposes, as would have been right at his
age, he felt called upon to answer his mother's need. By one of the
almost unbelievable devices of young hurt life, he took it upon
himself to become her knight, confessor and protector and, in a
very practical way, tried to bring order into the chaotic household
which, if I may say so, reflected her state of being. He thus
attempted a maturity which put him out of step both within himself and with other boys. His mother to him was fascinating and
helpless, mysterious and unpredictable, and in the relationship
with her he felt needed, wanted and of value. Whatever fulfilment
it gave him—and this, indeed, was great, for it meant becoming his

father in the eyes of his mother—the sense of deprivation of his
natural boyhood life during this period, of a healthy view of himself, was immense. For unlike myself, the therapist, he could have
no idea of how it all came about, namely as a balancing way of self-
preservation. The relationship to his mother was as frustrating to
his ego as it conferred upon him a significance and a value disproportionate to his age. The attraction and fulfilment were so
strong and so compelling that they activated, but also absorbed, too
much of his energy, leaving his natural instinctual self hungry,
unsatisfied and deeply resentful, as well as preventing critical
areas of his personality from maturing. If one can feel with him
this conflict, this severe disruption, it will give an inkling of the
sense of need and urgency which brought him to analysis and
enabled him to devote his energy, time and money to maintaining it.

In a unique way, the unlived, the missed years of his life came
up one by one when he was ready for them, when they found in
outer life a corresponding situation or person that seemed to
reflect them.

The engineer experienced a particular fascination for boys of
around eight-years-old, which was as inexplicable to him as it was
alarming. He feared to be homosexual. However, what he had
missed at about this age had been vital parts of his own development, and these moments of his unlived eight-year-old boyhood
were activated when he saw boys of that age expressing themselves.
When we reached the first critical stage, one point of damage came
up after the other: his vitality, self-valuation, self-assuredness, his
undoubtedness, his validity and his spontaneity. These qualities
created in him such a yearning to participate that when he saw
a boy skipping and dancing down the road, he, the thirty-year-old,
had to hold himself back not to do likewise. From this we may
gather how he must have felt in the playground when all the other
boys, as well as his younger brother, seemed to be buoyant and
active in the joy of life, with him as the odd man out.

These suspended portions of the ego are registered only by the
fascination experienced by seeing them outside. They rightfully
belong to the potentially healthy ego, but not having been evolved
at their natural time of growth, they are not felt as belonging to
oneself and so project themselves. As an example, the outer eight-
year-olds were the engineer's own second cousins. They were
healthy, self-reliant boys and strongly resisted the older man's
identifying with them when swimming, climbing, playing, etc.

A somewhat similar experience that led to a decisive improvement in his ability to handle such fascinations occurred in

Switzerland on a skiing trip. The engineer met a girl of thirteen
in the group they were skiing with, he got caught in teenage play
and high spirits, as if he were a boy of that age, and for the first
day or two it went well. But on the second or third day, this young
girl palled up with another teenage girl, and the two of them were
laughing at him and making fun of him. He came to realise that
the girls sensed that his attitude and expression, though appropriate for thirteen, were strange and rather odd for someone old
enough to be their father. This time, instead of going into despair,
he was able to spot this activation of his younger side himself and
to some extent sort it out straightaway, and thus recovered his
morale.

You may have noted that in this case he identified himself with
a girl; throughout his analysis, the feminine counterparts of the
younger ages with which he reunited within himself would sooner
or later emerge. This is very significant, demonstrating first of all
that he is far from being a so-called homosexual. Furthermore, his
psychological development illustrates the biological fact that any
human being is basically male and female but for a very small
quantum that determines whether the individual will be launched
into its lifespan as a boy or girl. In Duncan's regrowth, we can see
that not only biologically but also in mind and spirit man com-
bines the potentialities of both male and female, and this suggests
that he has an unusual capacity for becoming whole and healed.

The working through in analysis of the significance of the 'ski-
girl' enabled the engineer to differentiate further his adult part,
the ego, from the fascination and pull of the younger ones, so that
he noticed more and more when he was going too far off age.
What he needed to relate to and get activated in himself was not
the actual young girl as such but the feeling a boy of fourteen
would experience when meeting such a girl, a feeling of buoyancy
and high spirits, playfulness and zest of life, in one word, the
quickening of his young manhood. This fourteen-year-old phase
had never been lived sufficiently. With his own giving attention
to, or what I call parenting, those suspended phases and ego parts,
the outer fascination lost its compulsive quality and the projection,
taken back and brought into his own present-day flow of life,
markedly increased his vitality and stamina.

This spirit of the fourteen-year-old enters into all of him, as a
new glow, a new liveliness. His step changes, versatility, initiative,
a fresh quality of life and living come into being. These qualities,
moreover, appear not only when the feelings of a fourteen-year-
old can be expressed, but even on the most adult occasions there

is this resonance, a change in the health, in the radiations of this man.

One after another, unlived ages of life down to four and up to fifteen and later emerged, and once he had some security in a particular age, its feminine counterparts appeared, in dream figures or attached to memories of the past. Through experiences in outer reality he gradually learnt to deal with his fascination.

I will give, from his own notes, one example, out of many impressive ones, of the important stages of winning back some aspect of the child within with its locked-up dynamic energy, which is experienced as the reunion of the ego with a suspended part of the personality.

For some days the engineer had felt contact with what he called 'the younger one'. This to him was a very big experience, a state of renewal, of newbornness, filling and warming the whole of him. This younger one in him seemed to get tired easily, in his words, 'like a new-born calf, a bit dazed and uncertain and not quite safe on its legs'; it had 'great wonder and intensity and then, rather like a child, wanted to go off to sleep'.

He had been together with this younger part within himself for several days, with a feeling of himself vitalised by that age, both personally and in his work. On the other hand, he too got easily tired. But he became quite upset because he found his sleep was being disturbed.

Then one day he came to his session much brighter. He had found out how he could deal with his sleeplessness. Following up some suggestions of mine, he had talked to this part of himself—indeed he had acquired a great facility of intelligently, maturely but most naively talking to those suspended aspects. He had discovered that his restlessness was really, as it were, the younger one trying to get near him. Thus, when instead of resisting this discomfort and taking a sleeping drug, he concentrated on and held the restlessness with great care, devotion and adult consciousness, then it was as if the younger one materialised. He sensed his presence and began to feel him, first his toes, then his feet, his legs, his knees and finally his whole body, until gradually the young one became incarnate. Then the embodied young man merged with him, the adult one, with great intensity and feeling; he eventually could relax and go to sleep. I was greatly impressed when within the same week a woman patient told me of a similar inner reunion.

At another time the engineer told me more about such an experience: 'It was a tingling all over my body, and it was as if the tingling one were a different person that takes over my body, like a shadow form takes over all my muscles and a tingling takes over, grips my muscles and becomes him. This new thing, him, is the same as me, only it is a third one.'

There are evidently two that have come together, and a trans-cendent 'he' who has come into being as their synthesis. He goes on: 'It is as if the new thing is my young side, coming into its own, getting embodied in and united with me. That is, the shadow person or form has now become the young one. It is very impor-tant for me to feel this in my body and limbs. In the early stages, now some months or even years ago, the first presented itself in dreams. Then, when the reunion took place, there was a paroxysm in my limbs as this took over, something takes over and the some-thing that takes over brings about this effect, this paroxysm in my limbs.'

I have given you the description of this experience of healing in depth, of regrowth, in his own words which in a man of uncommon ease and facility of expression still reflect a groping for words to convey an experience that all but defies verbal expression. It is a transforming moment of life, a moment of consummate fulfilment and highest significance. And yet this is something which, like any new phase of growth, has to be experienced again and again, over a period of time, in different circumstances, until it is well rooted, undoubted, complete, secure.

Superficially, one might feel that we are here confronted with a de-personalisation in a schizophrenic process, with a fragmented personality. But actually we are dealing with something entirely different, with the regeneration of the ego under the auspices of the self, whereas the schizophrenic is in a state of disintegration and his ego is more or less overwhelmed by the powers of the unconscious.

In order to counterbalance the consuming concentration on, and strain of bringing about, the opus, people such as the engineer need the discipline of daily work, to some extent comparable to the demands of the psyche. It means attending to dreams at three a.m. and still getting up when the alarm clock goes by seven a.m. to go to work.

The constant check for the analyst in this specially exacting and unpredictable work is whether and how the patient's inner and outer world respond to this endeavour. In those who are called upon to undertake this journey, we arrive at a paradox: in order to reconstitute the ego by reuniting it with those suspended parts of earlier development, the self must be present already in a kind of shadowy prefiguration or awareness — it might also be called integrity—so as to enable the ego to reach its rightful state. (In analysis, the ego more often forms the starting point for the emergence of the self.) Otherwise it would not be possible to combine the mutually exclusive and seemingly self-contradictory requirements of this work: an attitude of receptivity of the ego which might also be described as creative emptiness, and a widely awake, intensively conscious concentration. Before the union of the adult ego with the younger part can be brought about, the ego needs the ability to relate to the younger in what I have called mature naivety, while maintaining its adult adaptation and persona. Such mature naivety, I believe, can reach down to where nature operates without consciousness, down to where growth takes place—it has to get near to that depth for regrowth to occur. At the same time, mature naivety is the foothold for the divine from where the ego can link up with the self: this, to my mind, recalls Jung's discovery of the symbol of the divine child— here it is received and honoured.

Hence it is not surprising to me that a religious sense or awareness is sooner or later emerging, an ability to tune in to a religious wavelength or what the engineer, in his electronic terminology, would call a religious frequency. Religion is the mystical and ritual way of the humble mortal to be in personal, not collective, relationship with the self. This religious sense has not necessarily to do with institutional religion as such, it would rather seem to be the original springs themselves, the vision out of which the institution once arose. We find it as something inherent in the human being, comparable to his capacity to receive wavelengths of colour, sound, light, etc., its sensitivity varying in different people. The engineer, for instance, was not what one would call a religious man. He had had some sort of formal religious education in his youth, without belonging to any particular Church, and yet it is remarkable and almost awesome to see that in moments of anguish and despair in the integration process, he would say the Lord's Prayer with the most concentrated attention. He remarked that to him the most essential phrases were: 'Thy Kingdom come; Thy will be done.' As he once put it: 'It relates me to my middle,' or, as we may add in Jungian terminology, taking the Kingdom of God as a symbol, to the self.

This repeated and anxious calling on God, out of the depth of his being rather than from the habit of religious teaching, indicates the intensity engendered in this process of fusion of the younger with the older which the ego has to hold. The fusion, activating the nascent energy of life in its original budding stage, left this man, after it was achieved, with a heightened sense of well-being; although at the moment physically exhausted, he remained vitalised. We may recall well-known parallels in alchemy, in chemistry and nuclear physics, where a reunion of separated parts is also characterised by intense heat and release of energy.

Duncan became more and more able to differentiate between his own inner figures and their counterparts in the outer world which before had exerted such fascination, such as his eight-year-old cousins and the skiing girl. A striking example of this capacity was his endeavour to recover for himself such qualities of his own younger brother as he felt he lacked. This younger brother, a happy-go-lucky type, did indeed carry the complementary extraverted shadow aspect of the engineer to an astounding degree. The struggle between them started early when Duncan was supposed to look after his brother and get him to school, but Tom would sit down in the road, no kicks or blows would move him, he had to be bribed with a pencil, a pocket knife or the like. He was stubborn and determined to have his way, independent and quite unmoved by expectations of mother, brother and others — in fact, he became a holy terror to Duncan. Later on, Tom went out with girls. Worst of all, through a common interest in football, he established a closer relationship with their father from which Duncan felt excluded. Thus there was a strong rivalry, almost a twin-brother situation, especially when Tom also joined the Scouts which Duncan felt were his own proper and exclusive territory. When grown up, the two brothers became good friends, helping each other with their complementary abilities and skills, Tom with business advice, Duncan with assisting him to sort out his sometimes rather mixed-up affairs with the opposite sex.

To Duncan, Tom was an important inner figure. In a dream, this brother gave him 'the belt of manhood', which we may translate as symbolising the archetypal qualities of maleness. The rather fantastic situation arose that, while Duncan in his analysis had reached the point where he had recognised his inner Tom and related to him, evolving a common name made up of his own and his brother's, Tom turned up at his flat to stay with him as a visitor. It will give an idea of the precision and clarity with which he differentiated between this inner complementary half and his actual brother, if I mention that one Sunday morning he had just decided that he wanted to be alone with his inner Tom and go out for a walk with him, when his brother came into the room and said: 'Let's go for a walk, Duncan,' which he regretted he just could not do as he had to attend to something else. Tom felt puzzled and offended by meeting in Duncan his own stubbornness and determination.

The consistency with which the engineer learned from his analysis to differentiate between his inner figures and their counterparts in outer reality, he gradually was able to apply in everyday situations, as a few instances may show.

His predecessor in his present job still had an office next door but was engaged in a different branch of the firm. They were good friends. One day, Duncan arrived for his session with me very despondent because he had taken the draft of some project to his colleague who would say: 'Yes, this is good, but what about here and what about there?' with the result that Duncan felt dejected and inferior until, during our analytical work, he could see that his colleague could criticise the project and extend its scope only because he was actually standing on Duncan's shoulder, that is, he was using the draft to add some of his own ideas to it. This taught the engineer to honour his own ego achievements more, as against his previous dependence on other people's judgments.

While in this case my assistance was still needed to balance his self-depreciation, you will see in the next example, slight in itself but a milestone as an experience, how he became capable of doing it himself.

He was playing tennis with two younger men of about twenty, and his play was upset by his consciousness of their difference in age. Then he noticed that his opponent was playing quite unself-consciously in a very individual style. At last he said to himself: 'Why not play *my* own way instead of playing up to the expectation of others?', i.e. with the idea of what his partners might be thinking of him. With this realisation, his game improved and his relationship to the two young people became much freer and easier.

A further, decisive, step of this development which made the engineer less dependent on the opinions of the outer world may be shown in his relationship with his chief, one of the leading executives in his particular field of industry. Since his analysis, Duncan had been selected for his present, highly specialised job. This involved having to attend to detail whilst keeping in view the total field—he had been picked out by his chief for projects which combine an imaginative approach with sound assessment of business possibilities as, for instance, an estimate of how many engines of a particular type would be likely to be required throughout the world by 1980. This required great inner security because there was no way of proving it in outer reality while, at the same time, a great risk and responsibility was involved because his forecast might influence the investment of millions of pounds.

Although his chief maintained the relationship of chief and junior, there was a good human atmosphere between them. On one occasion when he, Duncan, became fascinated by a project of his own, the boss said: 'That's a good idea, but don't you think you are rather overselling it?' Duncan took this with good grace, without feeling unduly dejected or hurt. Soon afterwards, when something very similar happened to his chief, Duncan was free enough to differentiate between the overemphasis of his chief on this project and its genuine merits. He handled the situation with a wise maturity, guiding the chief while keeping his own insight into his bias well to himself.

Having thus maintained himself over against a strong father figure, he then became able to establish an adult and human relationship with his mother—the most difficult of his achievements, because she was at the root of his deepest hurt. He went back home periodically to see her, which now was nearly always fruitful, whereas previously it used to be very upsetting. Recently his mother was telling him of her younger married days and said that she had been very fond of a Mr. A., adding: 'I thought of going away with him, but I never did.' The son replied: 'I never thought for a moment that you would.' The mother replied: 'Why, didn't you think I was human enough for it?' Then Duncan suddenly realised to what extent he had been viewing his mother as an idealised image. This realisation came with a good deal of impact and brought him a much-needed sense of differentiation, the lack of which had previously obscured the reality of the human being his mother was and, accordingly, had misguided him in his approach to and his expectations of women as such. I would like to add that there is an interesting paradox. Duncan knew through his terrible early experiences full well that his mother was hopeless as a responsible parent. Yet she represented, up to this moment, the image of the ideal, can we say, archetypal woman and mother.

The relief which this insight brought has been followed by an experience of central importance, the relationship with a young woman of his own age when his total being could come to life and meet the response of his chosen partner. After so many years of combined, devoted work it was gratifying to hear that healing in depth had really taken place: he could marry and take on himself more and more such problems as arose in his daily life.

The analyst's hygiene

As in all such deep work, special attention has to be paid to the therapist's own inner hygiene. When we who are workers in this field deal with other human beings without being sufficiently aware of our own place of hurt and need, we are actually using this most sensitive critical place of our own as a tool, an instrument, and do not give it its own rightful recognition and care. We may think we are working securely behind a wall of objectivity, but sensitive 'personalness' is passing through this permeable wall of our psyche. It is this which directs us and takes us to those aspects of our work which carry the glint of fascination — or its opposite, resistance, maybe even repulsion. If we are working with such an intensely personal part of ourselves without knowing it, without conscious awareness, we are bound to be damaged severely.

On the other hand, if we, the analysts, have been through a comparable experience and challenge, if the child within us has been discovered, acknowledged and enabled to take part in the whole adult personality, then we will not unknowingly project our own needs on to the patient. Moreover, the healing quality within us therapists will be of a different, convincing order. For, being in a positive relationship within ourselves to that which we are trying to heal in others, has in itself a healing effect.

Control cases

Checking and supporting my own experience, I have found that this conception of the critical hurt and the feed-back to damaged areas, often personified, was felt to be helpful both by colleagues to whom I told it, and by trainees of mine who applied and tested it in their own line of work. I will quote part of a letter and of a report which I received from a young psychiatrist, a woman of thorough scientific education. In her work she is using the utmost of her consciously acquired knowledge, training and experience. Before Jung's discovery of synchronicity, occurrences such as she records were treated as outside the modern scientific laboratory situation, as esoteric experiences or just some rather doubtful wobbliness in the worker, whereas now they can be taken seriously; one might even say that a scholar is no longer truly scientific unless this 'otherness' is taken into consideration and included. Perhaps I might add that her approach is a representative example of that mature naivety previously referred to, combined with a modern outlook. Here is her letter:

I am sending you these little notes on experiences with the

influence of 'inner children' on my psychotherapy. This interaction has occurred for a far longer period. I remember that
it used to be a very disturbing factor. There was a time early
in my own analysis when I, or rather the unsatisfied needs in
me, became very jealous of my patients, for instance of a mother
who had many nice children, or of any children who developed
well. Everything became very mixed up, I, the patients and the
inner children.

Then came a period, after I started work with you, when I
became aware of the interaction and attempted to keep these
inner people separate from the patients. I allowed them to help
me but I did not then give them anything in return. During this
period I had success in getting to the right place with the
patient, but I myself got tired, and sometimes during the
course of treatment I lost the ability to create with the patient
the right situation for his own healing.

Only lately I came into the third phase of this interaction. I
became aware of the needs of my inner children and I talked to
them now and again within sessions [i.e. her own clinic sessions]
when my inner children became touched by the patient's
problem. I became aware that not only was there a stream going
from my own experiences and inner persons to the patient, but
also there was a stream back from the patient to me. I had, of
course, noticed this long before, but only as a disturbing
element which must be eliminated. Only since I have worked
with children in my work have I noticed that there is a good and
creative stream coming from the patient to me.

The last phase started only very recently, when you told me
about the writing you are doing. What I am learning now is to
allow these inner children to get what they need. The process is
then as follows:

1. When I meet a patient, something of my own inner
children is touched by his need. Because this is touched, I can
understand the patient and find the right words at a given
time.

2. When the patient's need touches my inner children, their
own need—the need of mine—is activated, memories come
back which have been hidden, colours and vividness.

3. This vivid memory has to be kept alive for a time within
myself, has to be increased. When that succeeds, I may find a
way in which I can fulfil what had been left unfulfilled or I can
at least get the feeling of the need and see how it can be fitted
into the whole of my person.

4. When that succeeds within myself, then something surprising happens in the patient. Because then, without one's doing, the patient finds a positive solution for his need or creates something which is a new way.

Here I should like to add that whoever is in his own centre might well constellate that in others.

Now—she goes on—almost every session in the day's work brings little bits here and there. And it is not only during actual work, it might come at any moment, as if the inner children are around all the time.

Of course, this is not new, it has happened always. What is new is only that one can catch these things like a spark and bring them into full consciousness. Is that the essence of any training in analytical psychotherapy?

This trainee enclosed the following notes on the influence of psychotherapy on the 'inner children', and vice versa.

When I saw the young patient, Joan, she was sixteen, wore plain clothes and did not care about her appearance. She had started work but had to leave it off because she had become afraid that the other girls would make remarks about her. I guessed that she had several pretty coloured scarfs and ties in her drawer but did not dare to wear them for fear that people would say: 'There, Joan is wearing new clothes.' She was surprised that I had guessed that, and next week she came in bright clothes and make-up. She soon started work again and went to dances.

I thought that I had helped Joan because I had been such a girl. I did not bother to help my own inner girl, though she often appeared in dreams.

The letter continues:

A few months ago I talked to Mrs. P., aged thirty. She had forgotten that she could 'feel' at the age of nineteen. She had left her inner girl behind in a village when she went away from there at about seventeen. Now we had to fetch that girl and join her with the married woman she is now. I knew about 'inner children' by then. I talked to her about the girl and we got her back. I talked with her about clothes. Then my own inner girl (aged about seventeen) said to me: 'What right have you got to talk to this woman about clothes when you do not help me?'

I thought I shall do that later, I was more interested in the way my inner girl helped me to do my work than in her own need which was increased when she had to help me treating these women. Mrs. P.'s girl came back when she bought her a pair of cheap earrings at a store, surprised about her low taste but naive enough to buy them. I thought that my girl had felt the same, but I had not allowed her then to be so childish.

Another patient, Pamela, was thirteen, and very sensitive. She was afraid of her growing womanhood and preferred to remain a tomboy. But it did not work and she withdrew. We talked about womanly things and parties. When Christmas came, she was ready to receive some girlish presents and showed them to me. We talked about cosmetics and clothes. My own inner girl became very restless, because she wanted to be taken care of, but I still did not notice that she also needed something herself and was not only there to help me in my work. It was through Pamela that I first had to listen to my inner girl because there was a similarity between the two: the tomboy, the shyness, the sensitivity.

During that period there were dreams relating to the need of my inner girl: several about having washed my clothes but having to let them dry. Within the next two months I had the following dreams:

I was going with Dr. Barker to a certain place to meet people and I am well dressed, a new coat, well-fitting.

I am with a group of well-dressed, distinguished people.

I have to dress an important infant with great care.

I have done some work and wear old clothes. I have to meet the royal family in order to tell them something.

I tell a friend that she now can wear red because she is older, but she tells me black would be more fitting.

I have to meet the Queen tomorrow.

This last dream occurred before I went shopping because I had to buy a hat and a skirt in order to go for an interview. I had thought about that, but it was the girl within who made this into an occasion, and the dream of having to meet the Queen made it real. The girl wanted to have something wild, I had to explain to her and argue with her that I have to consider my age and status. One has to make a compromise between the desire of the girl who had her femininity disturbed and wants everything now, and my own needs to have the appearance which suits my inner feelings and social position. The girl and I continued to argue and she caused me to have a sleepless night. She said that she wanted to have nice clothes and that I had enough money to buy them. I argued that I have to drive in a dirty old car and play with children with paint and sand, also I have no space for new things. But the girl spoke from a depth, that was after meeting Dr. Barker yesterday, and we came to an agreement, we became one during the night and there was peace. I told her this morning she can choose what to wear and we would talk it over every day together. She now gets the attention and guidance she had missed, every time we have to meet over work.

The next report reads:

I saw a woman aged thirty, called Dorothy. She had a poor and unhappy childhood and had felt that she was of no value to anyone. She had shabby clothes when at school and did not dare to go anywhere. I showed her that I understood the feelings of her childhood. Then my own little girl was there, little Anne, at the ages of six, eight, eleven, thirteen. They all came together. They talked about their clothes, mother had always dressed her different from others, a bit too arty, not chic enough. Then came poverty after the war and one could not invite anyone. There was a birthday party and Mother gave her a present to take to the girl who was very rich. The present was not new, it had been an Easter egg and now was filled with new chocolates. When the poor egg was lying there on the friend's birthday table, together with far richer presents, Anne felt very downhearted and resolved that parties were silly, not really for her anyway. She did not know what the fashions were like and she could not dance. All this came back vividly now when we talked with Dorothy. So the little girl felt lonely and wants to have more friends now, perhaps a home where one can make them welcome. I had to tell her that she has to wait a little until I get a job which permits me to make a home. But I feel with her and give her my sympathy now.

Dorothy told me that her legs were too fat and she always had been afraid to walk in front of people. We looked at her legs and thought they were not so bad. My little girl looked too, then later she thought of her legs and that they never had been as she wanted them to be and she had always been afraid to walk in front of other people, indeed she never wanted to be seen walking. Then something happened to the legs. I took lessons in movement, and we were asked to improvise to music. Suddenly it seemed as if no more ideas came from the upper part of the body, all had got into the feet, it was as if the sense of movement had got down into the legs. This happened a fortnight ago. When I told the teacher, she replied that was right, she had been waiting for this.

Today we met Dorothy again. I had asked her to make dolls' clothes for my clinics, so that she may feel her inner child again. She made the clothes but could not feel yet. So we dressed the doll, I, Dorothy, my inner child and the faintness of Dorothy's inner child. We looked at the doll, and then Dorothy remembered her big doll who lost her legs in transport so that she never got her whole. And my inner girl suddenly remembered her big doll (when aged three) who later got a damage to the left leg, so that it was always shorter than the right one and nobody could repair it. We both, Dorothy and I, became very sorry for the little girls who had to love the dolls with their damage. I wondered then whether this damage of the doll has to do with the feeling of damage of one's own leg, whether the sadness about one's own imperfect body is linked to that of the imperfect doll.

WIDER APPLICATIONS

In encouraging and supporting a healing process by directing the adult's consciousness to those suspended personalities of an earlier age, I feel I got nearer to the process of growth and re-growth, of healing, than ever before. From the scientific point of view, I regard such experiences as most valuable opportunities for *research* and discovery of hitherto unrevealed aspects of the human psyche.

The labour put into this work and the resulting attitude, apart from being worthwhile in themselves, will also help one with other patients who are not fated to travel the length and depth of the whole journey.

The insight I had to gain, the ways and sensitiveness I had to develop, have helped me to see in much *milder but more concealed cases* a similar process at work and to go more assuredly and quickly to such key places where real healing could be achieved.

In what I should like to call *short-term treatment* I have found my conception helpful for the immediate relief of tension in acute anxiety states, in dealing with suicidal tendencies and stress leading to severe somatic pain. The therapist's insight into the basic pattern of recurrence will, if grasped by the patient, often bring almost spontaneous alleviation to the sufferer, beyond that of an ordinary abreaction.

I might mention here that I had a patient of sixty-eight who had had a deep interest in Jung's psychology for over thirty years. After about one year of personal analysis, though scattered, she came to see me much later for some deeper insight into herself rather than for prolonged treatment. During a very few conferences, in which I used this conception, I found a central critical hurt in her life. Her personality had been dislocated at twelve, when her mother died and her father married the governess. I had recognised the glowing young person which at sixty-eight was still there in her, and could help her to relate to her, and this served to heal an injured strand in her life. She said it was the first time in her experience of analytical approach that she felt linked up in some way, and that now the concept of the shadow had made sense to her. Most of all, these few sessions brought her a feeling of peace and serenity she had not felt before.

In *long-term treatment* I have applied this conception to very disturbed and isolated patients, including one who needed mental hospital care, with results that suggest that further application to such severe cases would be a promising line of research.

Beyond the clinical field there is a far *wider area* in everyday life, where this conception may help to understand people one meets more deeply and comprehensively; but this would be an investigation of its own.

V

The Religious Cord

V

**THE CRISIS OF BELIEF. CONTRIBUTIONS FROM PHYSIOLOGY AND
PSYCHOLOGY**

There is a moving place in Jung's television film *Face to Face* when
John Freeman asked him, 'Do you believe in God?' After an
almost painful pause in which Jung's face had the look of utmost
concentration, he replied with a smile: 'I don't have to believe — I
know.' This differentiation between belief and knowing is of
critical significance for modern man and his well-being.

The crisis of belief

Up to about the sixteenth century, the relationship to the powers
of creation was mediated in the Western world by the Bible, interpreted and organised by the Church. There was no hesitation, no
doubt on the whole, in accepting this presentation literally and
all-embracingly. All arts, philosophy and the so-called sciences
were contained in it.

The first rupture of this conception of the world was the discovery on the side of natural science when Copernicus and Kepler
established that the earth moves round the sun, i.e. that the earth,
man's Earth, was not the centre of the universe as had hitherto
been believed. It is difficult to realise now what an utter dis-
placement of what we would call today ego security was thus
started.

Another great shock occurred much later, when Darwin, himself
an earnest Christian, demonstrated the development of the human
species out of the animal world, showing that man and apes had a
common ancestry, thus shaking at one stroke the feeling of man
being specially created by God himself. As level-headed a man as
Disraeli said at the time that he would rather be on the side of the
angels than on that of the apes.

The similarly shattering geological discovery of the stratification of the earth demonstrated visually and undisputably its immense age from the fossil remains the strata contain. Here was an almost atomic explosion, an expansion of time from the under six thousand years of the accepted biblical age of the world to five thousand million—time beyond human grasp—putting the Christian geologists into an impossible position. A distinguished one brought ridicule upon himself by maintaining that, as God had only seven days to make the world, He must have created it, as it were, ready-made with its stratifications and fossils.

Up to my grandfather's time, 'spontaneous generation' was taken for granted. It was so obvious to demonstrate, you only placed old rags and some cheese in a dark corner, and not infrequently, after a certain time, the rags brought forth mice. Even simpler was the ocular demonstration that meat could generate worms out of itself, giving a semblance of scientific basis to the possibility of generation out of nothing. The development of new insights into zoology disproved this theory, thus rendering the belief untenable on a scientific plane.

These dramatic revolutions in man's view of life on this earth and his feeling of himself set up a terrible tension in many an honest soul, undermining as they did the literal interpretation of the Bible. Man became crucified, could we say, between the alternatives of either disowning his hard-won reason and so maintaining his belief in God or else abandoning his God in order to be true to the objective facts. It is hard to grasp how recent many of these developments are, indeed very little older than the internal combustion engine and the aeroplane at the turn of this century. We are still experiencing the reverberations of this challenge. The old, literal, blind belief in the Bible, which for so long brought spiritual comfort, security, hope and meaning to the community as a whole, is still desperately hung on to by isolated communities and so-called fundamentalists, but most likely with an ever-increasing loss of mental honesty and integrity.

Belief in science

On the other hand, science as such has not been able to bridge the gulf that has arisen, let alone replace the steadying effect of the experience of God. There was indeed a time in the nineteenth century, in the first moments of freedom from literal dogmatics, when science seemed to hold the promise of security in the newly-found laws of nature which were then regarded as unchangeable and immutable—qualities hitherto held in the image of God—

science thus almost taking the place of religion, and that with a vision of continuous progress. In our time, however, with the invention of finer and more precise instruments and ever-increasing specialisation in every branch of science, what seemed to be a simple, clear and final truth of say a molecule has become a complex, almost infinite variety of its components — so where is security gone? As a scientist friend said to me the other day, looking at what until recently was the invisible speck called the virus through an electromicroscope with its possible million-fold magnification, this speck of matter was not only now visible but seemed to have grown into the size and complexity of a whole township — so where is definiteness gone?

Hence even science, as a new hope for security, no longer holds good because, instead of bringing us a basis of final, reliable facts, it shows an immense and ever-increasing diversity of unknown facts and factors. Thus where religion no longer seems to carry, science, after almost taking its place, has now, in its turn, proved to be neither final nor unchangeable in its findings. Where is there firm ground for the individual to stand on and relate to in this fast-moving and ever-shifting world?

We have indeed been rocketed out of the medieval pattern of undoubtedness into a new and ever-expanding orbit of ideas and observations which we can hardly comprehend yet nor have had time to adjust to. Not least, there is a disturbing sense of weightlessness impinging on us, but weighting ourselves with material objects and possessions we find to bring only transitory relief, as if our centre of gravity had lost its magnetism. With the most honest endeavour, we are confused, disorientated. It is not surprising, then, that people, out of the feeling that there is nothing to believe in, of insecurity and insignificance, look desperately for new ways, including all sorts of substitutes for religion.

The need of belief

This poses the question why man is so much in need of belief or, in our language, of his own personal relationship to what we might call the transcendent. This need seems to be as old as man himself. In order to grow onward healthily, he has to feel his relationship to his ancestors and at the same time have a vision of his way to go forward, so as not to disintegrate or be eaten up by blind collective powers and fears. It seems to be a human necessity to have an awareness of the mystery of where one comes from and whither one is going. Prehistoric caves show pictures which have been interpreted by palaeontologists as medicine men or shamans who, up to today, carry the role of mediator between man and the powers greater than he. In early sun worship the sun was taken as the eternal centre and source of life to which sacrifices were offered. In all religions, from the most primitive to the highly developed, rituals maintain the reciprocal relationship between man and the beyond, that from where we come and towards which we are orientated. As long as these rituals still carry reality, secure the sense of continuity, of orderedness and maintain the relationship to the transcendent, there is no problem or dilemma, because then one is held as a member of a tribe or group.

It is only in recent times that rituals increasingly appear to have lost this power of communication over a wide area and no longer carry their transcendent meaning, despite the earnest endeavour of organised religions. We are no longer contained in the Garden of Eden situation of our own creation myth, nor else, like a bird, living in its natural order, guided by instinct on how to build a nest, where to go in autumn and how to return in spring. Now we need to use this self-same consciousness which originally activated the scientific search and, with it, brought doubt and insecurity, to recover the awareness of our kinship with the powers beyond in which and through which we have our being. This means a new approach to the basic, archetypal, powers, those royal and eternal presences, so as to release their everlasting and yet ever new life-bringing significance.

Scientific facts strengthening the religious cord

As one of those who cannot believe blindly, I would like to take you to some of the realms where I have found evidence of order and directedness which we so desperately need for our well-being, to facts that may help us to relate to what I have called the religious cord or wavelength. I will give some examples from science itself, from the realm of physiology and embryology, as well as from psychology, which may recover the sense of awe and wonder, reinforce and stabilise belief from the side of modern scientific findings.

Even in the seemingly simplest forms of matter and life, such as vitamins and viruses, a highly intricate order is found which merges into the ordered symmetry and prefigured arrangement of atoms such as in the lattice of crystals, the most ordered forms of existence we know so far.

The wonder of healing

Let us consider now something known to all of us: a cut of the finger. With reasonable care, we expect that this will heal in a relatively short time, and the finger be restored to its healthy condition. We call it simple, but when you go into it, the subtlety of healing is almost beyond our comprehension. As soon as the finger is cut, a fantastic diversity of precise activities is set into motion. Messages to and from the brain, acquainting the organism with the exact state of affairs at any given moment, are carried by messengers, the hormones, bringing about a complicated first-aid system through the supply of blood, the change of blood cells, the increase of clotting time, even before the regrowth of tissue and the assembly of all the constituents necessary for it—a concerted effort which far exceeds the complexity and efficiency of the most modern operating theatre.

From cell to embryo

For each of us, however, probably the greatest wonder which all of us have experienced but none remember is our own development from a single cell to the immense complexity which we each of us had reached when we were born into this life. It is an amazing fact that of all the eggs that our mother shed, this particular one should be met at this special moment by the one sperm of the hundred thousands that our father had mediated, and so bring about the very me and not one of my sisters or brothers, the individual persons as which we find ourselves. Although the main stages of development have been mapped out in the science of embryology in seemingly great detail, yet like the revelations of the ultramicroscope, they confirm what all great scientists now agree on, that absolute comprehension of the subtle orderedness of this development, as well as that of the universe, is beyond human comprehension and most likely ever will be. It is only recently that the part of the 'controlling enzymes' has been discovered, those invisible entities which will slow down or speed up some particular cell growth, so that this fits exactly into the growth and timetable of the developing whole. Moreover, on this journey from the single cell to the moment of our infant entry into this sunlit world, we pass through the main phases of ancestral development, aeons of cosmic time condensed into those few months, thus being most basically initiated into terrestrial existence and so belonging to, even having a blood kinship to, the whole community of life on this earth. In that original single cell there must be a system of potentials which prefigures all the characteristics that become manifest later and which in the nine months of development, each in its turn, takes its ordered place in the evolution of the embryo, with a precision of timing infinitely greater than in the most complicated feats of human construction. This precise, ordered development is perhaps easiest grasped when something goes wrong, as it sometimes does once in one of so and so many million times: that the heart is on the right side instead of the left, the fingers or toes are too few or too many, two seams do not close, we have a hare lip, or brachial gill slits of our fish-developing days do not completely close and we have a partial slit or cyst in the side of our neck. But the astonishing thing is that, under ordinary circumstances, everything goes right.

The organiser

What is evident, however, to all who have studied these phenomena, is that there must be a central power who not only shapes and forms from the fertilised egg the embryo into a human being, that is, with the necessary collective traits and statistically correct measurements that are called human, but beyond this creates an individual person every time, each organ of which is unique to him or her: no two bony structures, no two kidneys are identical. Every mother knows that, however many children she has had, each is different, as are the fingerprints of all of us, and the uniqueness of all these innumerable variations must somehow have been contained in our original cell. This mystical central power responsible for the wonder of ordered growth and differentiation embryologists have called by the mundane name of the organiser.

Could we say, in an attempt to comprehend this order, that this numinous power, the organiser, brings about the development of the embryo by organising the various centres or dominants such as heart, lungs, liver, eye, nervous system, etc., each of infinite complexity but all united in obedience to this mystical power? Analogously, we could think of the psyche as being organised under the auspices of the self together with the whole hierarchy of archetypal centres or powers.

Looking back on the astounding fact that, from the moment of conception, the embryo, be it of an animal-to-be or a human-to-be, develops in an ordered way and, if no hitch occurs, will become a complete representation of its species; realising, moreover, that even after the birth into this world, the orderedness and care are not lost, as we have seen for instance from the cut finger, we may have got some grasp of the factual existence of a great power behind the development and maintenance of life on this earth. To me, one of the profoundest wonders of all is that, with this abundance of growth, we, each of us, are in some mysterious way coined as individuals—so different from technical mass production. That this power should come to be called divine is to me scarcely surprising.

The psychological side

We will now see if we can find an equivalent of comparable order and caringness in the realm of the psyche. Jung, as a physician, has courageously explored the uncharted region of the soul. We, as his students, may have met, knowingly or unknowingly, the organiser of embryology in our dreams, in meaningful coincidences or in our experience of the broken cord of meaning being re-established in the course of personal analysis.

Dreams

We all have had dreams, we all may have been puzzled by coincidences, but to what extent, if any, did we look for observable signs of the great organiser, and if so, did we take them on? A sense of receptivity, of awareness, needs to be developed, a readiness to respond, otherwise it is like food passing through the guts without the tissues being able to take it up and to benefit from it; unless our tissues are permeable and mediate the extract appropriately into the body substance, we may starve in the midst of plenty, as in diabetes the blood becomes syrupy with sugar but the sufferer, more and more hungry for sugar, is at the same time starved of it to the point of death because the essential mediating factor, insulin, is not available.

Meaning

Similarly, a human being may feel that there is no meaning for him in his life, yet someone outside can see it around and about him, perhaps even in plenitude. But the awareness that there might be meaning for him and the readiness to accept the responsibility for what this entails needs not only to be discovered but accepted and loved. The receptivity for and the experiencing of meaning, and the reaction to it seems blocked and the visibility darkened by shadow aspects. We so readily hope that coming for analytical treatment means to be acted on and can replace our own active response. Or else we may look for guidance, for values, in the wrong way, expecting them always to come in a big way though often they will speak with a still small voice. Meaning will manifest itself very often in an irrational context, so that I have learned to look in the most irrational part of a dream for what I would call the logic of the unconscious. How often have we ourselves felt about a dream: 'This is nothing but a jumble, a silly fragment,' but when tuned to and decoded, it proved to be a key to a door that much needed to be opened? But we have to open it, then act, and this may bring a challenge which we long hoped to avoid.

Taking belief as a problem of modern man, of those fellow human beings who had and have to discover, may I say rediscover, the gods of old as a reality of their own inner selves, of psyche as the carrier of meaning, the pathfinder to our entelechy, we will try to look at manifestations of meaning. We will search for traces of the organiser of embryology, for his fingerprints, if I may say so, in our own life, so that we do not need to believe but can know from within and without. Even at moments of deep distress we can at least realise that there is a possibility of knowing, and thus have the hope and courage to continue actively in our endeavour.

Unless we look out for the organiser in our dreams, check on coincidences and psychosomatic happenings, explore whether or not they are meaningful, and so experience these encounters with the basic forces as a challenge, they may even appear at times as enemies of our one-sided wilful planning, if we fail to realise that they might be guides and friends, we may lose one of the greatest supports which Jung's discoveries can bring to us.

Examples from psychotherapy

I have chosen some examples from my daily work but also some drawn from other sources, so as to show that this is not just a subjective bee in my bonnet. Let us start with the world of dreams. First, what one might call a warning dream.

Warning and caring dreams

A man in his forties, at a precarious moment of outer and inner life, had the following dream: He was sitting in a smallish room. The only thing he could remember as being special was a cuckoo clock—a clock that calls out the hour. When asked what the time was, he saw that the clock had stopped, roughly between six and eight a.m. On association, the room became recognisable as that of a roadside café frequented by cyclists. He himself was at that time keen on cycling, including racing. In fact, he was to take part in a race in two days' time and, for this purpose, was having lighter handlebars fitted to his machine.

The analyst, alarmed by the clock having stopped in the dream, asked whether the dreamer felt safe to race, and when this was answered in the affirmative, enquired whether the mechanic could be relied upon to do the alteration properly. Taking the hint, the dreamer checked the machine before starting and was shocked to discover that a vital nut on the only brake of the machine had not been properly adjusted. Under the stress of racing, the brake would undoubtedly have failed, possibly causing a crash that might have been fatal for the rider. The race started at six a.m., and Time could well have stopped for him before eight a.m.

And now what one might describe as a caring dream.

A young doctor, interested in psychology but without personal experience of analysis, was at the most critical stage of a final post-graduate examination when he had the following dream. He was standing in a landscape with the sun just appearing above the skyline in front. In between him and the rising sun was a giant shadow figure, and as he pondered on it, the words came: 'Only you yourself stand between you and victory.' This dream so alerted him—feeling he would be damned if he stood in the way of his own success—that summoning all his concentration and resources, he succeeded in passing his examination. So he, too, took on his dream.

We have met a warning and a caring dream, one by a man under analysis and which needed careful decoding by analyst and analysand, the other by a man outside of analysis: it is evident that dreams indeed are not necessarily the outcome of analysts' expectations, as some psychotherapists seem to hold.

Synchronistic events

I would like to turn now to what Jung has called synchronistic events, those meaningful coincidences which we may all have experienced on a smaller or larger scale. The questions remain: what did they convey to us? how did we receive them? and how did we respond?

I myself, during my analytical work, experience not infrequently that some detail of what impressed me in a play I saw or in some bedtime reading, or in a periodical opened at random, may turn out next morning to convey insight into a clinical situation. Moreover, an unusual clinical occurrence in the morning is often unexpectedly repeated in the afternoon, a fact which I accept gratefully as a sign that I may be in Tao with the situation.

Meaningful coincidences, however, may happen not only to individuals but also to groups. An example of this occurred to a young psychiatrist who, as interpreter, conducted a party of Russian physicians on a medical tour of England. Unexpectedly having an evening off while at Liverpool, they decided to see a film and, with no idea of its contents, chose *Whistle down the Wind*, the story of children who felt they had found Jesus in a murderer who was transformed by their trust. There the atheistic Russians of this party, we can say 'met Christ' and were deeply moved by this encounter in their own way, despite all their indoctrination. We wondered what made them select the film.

As the next examples I have chosen events in the psychosomatic field, again two under analysis, one outside it.

Psychosomatic experiences

Regarding psychosomatic experiences, I would like to concentrate on one somatic symptom, asthma, which I have had a chance to observe in several patients. In each case, it was a young adult daughter who worked in London and whose widowed mother lived in the country. It was remarkable how not only visiting the mother, but even contemplating a visit, brought on a bronchial asthma attack, and it was striking how, when the insight into the significance of the physical symptom and its possible psychological meaning increased, what one might call an immunisation took place, so that a visit could be made without an attack. In one of the situations I remember, I suggested that the daughter should write down what she felt about her mother's good intentions and how she sensed, behind it all, selfishness and self-indulgence rather than the self-sacrifice the mother tried to make out. This the daughter did and wrote straight from the shoulder. I had expected it to be written in her dream book so as to be worked out analytically, but to my surprise and, I must admit, with a tinge of consternation, I heard that she had not only written it as a letter but posted it. However, the effect was most encouraging. Not only did the letter relieve the daughter's asthma, but I was glad to hear that the mother was courageous and humble enough to take it well, and thus the relationship of the two improved considerably.

Another young woman patient, after a considerable amount of treatment, took to spontaneous painting. Her pictures were in strong, basic colours and one could see the tempestuous surges of coloured cloud formations mirroring in a most realistic way the struggle going on within her, some showing the onset of constricting energy, others the stage of release. Looking at the pictures together and daring to feel the emotion they contained, gradually helped her to realise that beyond and behind her asthma attacks was the sensation of being sat on and squashed. In time, as the tie to the mother loosened, this sensation of being sat on was transferred from her to other people and situations, to a woman friend, her landlady or, finally, even the office. Eventually she came to see that she herself was the negative mother, sitting on herself. By now she is able to take the discomfort of an oncoming asthma attack as a possible indication of an inner situation, and by asking herself, 'What sits on me?' recognises the situation she is in. The imminence of an asthma attack could thus be experienced as a warning hint from someone inside her who cares.

As my third example of a psychosomatic experience, I want to mention the first disaster in Swiss aeronautical history when one of the stewardesses fell ill the night before her scheduled flight with a severe gastric upset. The doctor was called in and she was reported unfit for duty. No other inmate of the hostel she was staying at, all of whom had eaten the same food, showed any sign of food poisoning. I refer to the Caravelle which crashed soon after taking off: she was the only survivor of her team. In this case, naturally, we do not know what the young woman experienced or learned from it.

Negative and positive aspects of order and care

Lastly, I would like to communicate an analytical experience of what happens if order and care, these two great attributes of life, turn negative, and what may be brought about when they are recognised and can be dealt with. A young man around thirty, whom we may call John, was referred to me by his former analyst who moved from the area, because of the difficulty the patient had in holding down a job. He was highly gifted and exceptionally skilled in an advanced technical field, but what puzzled my colleague was that, while John had no difficulty in doing work well that did not interest him, though he would soon throw it up because of boredom, he would, on the other hand, not be able to hold a job where the work really fascinated him. Soon ideas of his own, often superior in creativity and appropriateness to those of his boss, would rush up as well as ways of organisation and practical application. Both, however, would result in a state of frustration, aggression and confusion, psychically to the point of feeling threatened by a superior when his ideas seemed to be rejected, often without basis in fact. Moreover, on the somatic side, light and seeing being of paramount importance in his work, physical symptoms would appear which included the sensation of impaired vision up to the terrifying fear of blindness.

In the course of intense and devoted analytical work we found that his complex reactions to his superiors mirrored experiences he had had with his father and his responses to them. His father was well-meaning but rigid and ruthlessly, even cruelly, dogmatic in trying to mould this talented elder son into the shape he thought he should be. So from early boyhood onwards he had suffered from the feeling that what meant most to him would be killed by his father. When older, the fear that whatever he wanted most to bring about might be steamrolled almost to extinction, was experienced most desperately with objects for which he cared especially. A wireless set he long wanted to have and purchased, a car which to him was just *the* car and which he could only afford because it needed repairs he knew he was well able to do, to his consternation 'turned hostile' while he worked on them, to such a degree that it would mean death to him to adjust some of the nuts and bolts. The death threat to anything that was his very own or precious to him became projected on these loved objects. These often shattering difficulties went on for quite some time. Taking up this type of situation together with analogous ones over a period of many months, brought him one day, after an analytical session, to the galvanising realisation that it was the negative father in him that was fighting him. He himself, together with the shut-off positive father within, thus became released and competent in the situation. With this relief transcending his previous disrupted state, he was able, after months of desperate attempts, to get the car repair completed within a few days.

To bridge a profound analytical development, I will refer to the occasion on which, in the outer world, he came up against his difficulties with his superior, in this case the director of a technical team. The situation was on the face of it a simple one: the team was shooting a film, and in his judgment the chief had placed a writing desk in an inappropriate position. His first reaction was that he dare not move it because of the resentment that he antici-pated. However, holding his centre and summoning his own inner, invisible authority, he could make the necessary adjustment, which turned out to be not only to his own satisfaction but was also accepted by his chief. Small as the occasion was objectively, his inner reaction was momentous. This experience enabled him to realise that he had a director within himself who was able to modify conditions and, in time, even to constellate people without evoking their wrath and without being destroyed but, on the con-trary, to the benefit of the actual situation. The discovery of the inner power which he came to call his invisible director strengthened him in holding his own in what would previously have been critically disturbing circumstances. When feeling related to this inner power, he could often not only protect his own ideas but tactfully and safely bring them into being when it was possible to do it. In time, he was even able occasionally to translate the messages expressed in his physical symptoms himself and act on them. I would like to mention that, by now, he has become the director of a team.

Freeing himself from the compulsion of his father's ideas of what he should be, and linking up with the positive father within consciously, to the point of being able to become a human director, the distorted, dislocated attitude could be repaired and this man be brought back nearer to his inborn pattern, to his lifeline. Living more in relationship with his own centre now, the director within, he has gained a sense of individual meaning. One cannot find one's meaning from a centre not one's own.

The strength of John's reaction in both negative and positive respects transcends ordinary volition, one's own will-power, and thus suggests that we are here in the realm of what Jung has called archetypes. It should be emphasised, however, that when, say, the personal father has had a too distorting influence on the individual in the growing period at a time when the parents are still felt as the carriers of the archetypal powers, then continued attention is needed because there is a marked sensitivity and lack of early adaptation, and a special awareness is called for whenever this realm is reactivated, as it is bound to be, in everyday life. It is not a 'once for all' but 'little by little' and 'on and on'.

The organiser and the father image

May I draw our attention here to the strange and impressive parallel between the organiser of embryology when it turns negative and the father image when it is experienced under a shadow aspect. When the organiser fails to control the total situation, we may have uncontrolled growth or malformation. Correspondingly, the great father image, negatively mediated and experienced as it was here through the personal father, may cause damage to the point of near-destruction where its true role is to protect and guide the young life. So far, we have not learned yet to contact the organiser of natural growth when he seems to be out of action. In the psychological field, however, where the terrestrial representative of an archetypal power has gone astray, there is the possibility of modifying the damage by the impact of a new, strong and wisely understanding relationship, to put it in general terms — in this case, first mediated anew by the analyst, and then taken on by the individual himself.

Daring to be open to the orderedness in the structure of matter and the wonder of growth, to the caring power we found in dreams, to psychosomatic symptoms, meaningful coincidences and the restoration of meaning in a human life, we met that power which the scientist has called the organiser, Jung the self, and a large part of mankind — God. The scientific knowledge that this power exists both centrally and individually may help to tune our attention and heighten our awareness so that, at some special moment, the transcendent experience may spark across the gap and so unite believing with knowing. We may draw encouragement from the words of the Delphic oracle which Jung lived with and responded to throughout his life and which he had carved over the doorway of his house in Küssnacht. They may be rendered: 'Called or not called, the god will be present.'

RELATING TO THE CENTRE
IN MEMORIAM C. G. JUNG

As a contribution to aspects of C. G. Jung's life and work which have a significant bearing on both the personal and professional level, I would like to speak about my own experience of what may be referred to as 'relating to the centre'.

Many years ago, when I treated a patient in a deep and prolonged depression, her manifest condition was such that I began to wonder whether the time had not come to give her the possible benefit of my E.C.T. machine. At this moment she brought a dream in which a light appeared in the midst of darkness, together with a helpful and admired teacher of her university days. With the patient's associations, this scene strongly suggested a manifestation of the guide of the soul, the *psychopompos*. The dream came as an utter surprise. There was nothing on the surface to indicate any positive movement or the possibility of it—she lived in black despair. Yet the dream showed that somewhere in her depth, near enough for her to relate to and consciously associate with, was a centre of light and help: dawn is born at midnight. With this encouragement I dared continue psychotherapeutic treatment, and soon after, an upward trend began which gradually led her out of her depression.

Years before, in my early days, while working in an observation ward and before I was much acquainted with Jung, I had come across the same kind of unexpected and helpful figures in dreams or phantasies of critically ill patients. The dramatic occasion mentioned above strongly reinforced my original experience that such dream occurrences can indicate that healing processes arise from the depth of the unconscious and, if the moment can be grasped by the therapist, the patient may gradually be led to conscious co-operation. Since then, whenever such a guiding or saving figure comes up in dreams, disguised maybe as conductor, gardener, etc., sometimes the same one reappearing at intervals of several months, I am naturally alerted, and if the patient is able to relate to its significance, this may bring him into more direct relationship with his centre, his lifeline or entelechy. Though such manifestations only occasionally take on a striking appearance, they have led me to recognise that we meet here a natural constituent of the psyche that is always there. It is for us, the psychotherapists, to ask which attitude one should strive for to become more appropriately sensitive to it. This has taught me to be on the lookout for, and to take note of, comparable movements in dreams and phantasies which were far less pointed.

These experiences with patients, together with my own inner experiences, co-ordinated and amplified by C. G. Jung's concepts and approach, have enabled me to realise that there is living within us a centre that acts like a great dramatist: it is as if, in response to life situations, it produces patterned radiations of energy which, like those from a television mast when received by a receptive instrument, appear as imagery on our own, highly selective, personal screen. If carefully decoded and related to with feeling understanding, these images can reveal a meaningful comment on a life situation, a caring concern that exceeds one's conscious grasp.

For all their ambivalence, dreams are a navigational instrument that can tell you how far you are off course. This imagery of the unconscious gives one the possibility of seeing the patient's truth, not only without undue conscious misinterpretations or prejudices but, as one might call it, stereoscopically from more than one angle. At moments of doubt in a patient's analysis I am most thankful not only when a dream appears but also for both the attitude and the instruments which Jung has brought to us analysts in the often very difficult and many-sided task of comprehending it. More than once I would have given up as hopeless the attempt to grasp the meaning of a dream or at least to obtain some guidance from it, without the morale — quite apart from the technical ABC — which one learns from the numerous interpretations throughout Jung's writings.

A patient's repeated experience that there is a centre within him that can and does create dream dramas, the scenes and characters of which evidence a knowledge of his past and present, sometimes even of future trends, with a subtlety and penetrative insight far beyond his or the analyst's, gives him the confidence that there is 'someone' within him who cares. This realisation brings nearer the possibility for him of feeling it safe to modify or lessen his dependence on the parental images and, last not least, on the analyst. The increased sense of a personal centre within may also diminish the need for an external absolute authority and thus, may lead to what one might call a more human conception of the great powers under whose auspices we live: in other words, he has a new chance to reach a more friendly reciprocal relationship with them, and with this, a release from an often confusing or distorting effect of early experiences of authority.

Those of us who worked under Jung at Küsnacht knew that while writing his books and teaching, he himself was all the time keeping in touch with his own inner world, taking care of his dreams and phantasies and working at his own problems and tensions. This came out impressively for instance in his Seminar* of 1925 and, as we now know, in the carvings and sculpture of his 'hideout' in Bollingen. This strenuous, often desperate endeavour arose out of a life necessity, not basically out of scientific interest, for his relationship to what we call the centre was critical for his sanity and his physical health, as so often he found himself in uncharted territory, at the fringe of the beyond. All this gave a sense of reality to his teaching and his writings, as well as a personalness which was a challenge to take on one's own task of relating to one's present-day conscious situation and its repercussions in the unconscious. It was then that one began to understand what was meant by 'work' in this context. For it seems that, without the individual giving the utmost, appropriate, endeavour to relate to the area activated by a dream and, if possible, comprehend the message it has brought within reach, nothing will happen.

In continuity with the age-old belief that dreams are messages from the gods, Jung re-emphasised their significance for the health of modern man. Beyond that, however, he more than most, was aware of the complementary realisation, namely—metaphorically speaking—how dependent the gods are on their relationship to individual human consciousness if they are to be creatively expressed or recognised on this earth. This is such a tremendous thought to me that although one is, in a sense, so insignificant compared to the gods, yet the individual has a significance which is indispensable to the gods. This realisation can take one out of forlorn isolation into a relationship of profound meaning, and if one can feel this being needed by the gods as oneself—not one's father or mother or sister or brother—then any human inadequacy becomes less important and falls into place. The more one is orphaned by early deprivation or distortion, the greater the need for such a relationship, the potential stimulus to find your own dynamic centre within. This takes one out of the childish immaturity and the victim role and forces one to transcend the infantile demands, for a parent relationship is not potent enough to live by for too long, however good they are or have tried to be.

However agnostic I may have been inclined to be in reaction to a strict dogmatic upbringing, such experiences have confronted me with the fact that there is a reality behind the more stylised representation of God in established religions. Behind the basic urge that brought about the religious rituals, the dramas

* See footnote to p. 20.

of belief, there was perhaps man's necessity to live in relationship to the mystery of his being—a dynamic sense of the continuity of his existence. This has a correspondence in the biological fact of the uninterrupted continuity from the beginnings of life on this earth. And being a microcosm of this evolution, we ourselves have built into us the experience of an unbroken development from the nucleus of the single cell at our conception into the unimaginable complexity of cells that make up our adult here and now.

One of Jung's great achievements is thus that modern man can re-relate to this centre, to the central mystery of one's being, without violating our hard-won rational faculty and experimental approach. I should like to add that the sense of the living existence of this centre within the individual and the endeavour to be orientated towards it gives me a better chance to rightfully direct myself to the patient's centre and thus, while holding my own, to relate to it constructively.

Apart from the challenge and stimulus to one's own endeavour which Jung's presence and example set, the effort one knew it took him and how he answered the conflicts and suffering life led him into, made one deeply respect him, but without the temptation to idealise him. To me, to idealise Jung is to depreciate him as a human individual by suggesting that he possessed some sort of superhuman powers or, at least, was so gifted that his achievements came to him without the efforts and the price that ordinary beings have to pay. We speak of hubris when man usurps the gods, but is it not another kind of hubris to project such powers upon a mortal, to reduce him to superhuman status as it were? Now that Jung is no longer with us in person, there is the danger that he might either become idealised or else blindly fought against, say as a father image—and such extremes would be an insult to his rugged humanness.

Index

ANALYTICAL CASES, *cont.*
Duncan, engineer, incompatible parents; example of healing in depth and regrowth, 140–51
Eleanor, senior welfare officer, critical hurt from mother's inhibiting influence; example of feedback, 119–27
gynaecologist, unrelated to her instincts, pioneer of birth control, 107
James, university teacher, attachment to mother blocks marriage, 111–14
Jewish man, mental disturbance ascribed to dental treatment; tracing the anima, 51–6
John, over-rigid father, crippling, discovers own inner 'director', 171–3
lawyer, woman, after abortions became qualified midwife, 107
mental patient, possessed by archetype of creativity, 46
Miss K. Y., psychotic breakdown, psychotherapy after discharge, 47–50, 67
Mrs. Somerset, chronic traumatising parental relationship, 99–105
professional man, brother's inhibiting influence, 69–70
'Round the bend', professional woman, suicidal tendencies, meeting inner figure of 16-year-old girl; example of recovering lost part of personality, 137–40

ANALYTICAL CASES, *cont.*
solicitor specialising in divorce cases, 107
woman, severe pain related to father's heart attack; example of feed-back, 117–118
woman, short-term treatment of critical hurt, 158
young woman creating family tensions in office, 98
young woman, unhappy love affair and abortion, founded home for unwanted children, 107
ancestral background, 63–5
anima, 26, 30–1, 40
imagery of, 54–5
positive and negative aspects, 51
tracing of, 51–6
animals,
as part of inner family, 74, 136
substitute parents, 81
sense of dignity, 78
trainers of, 78
animus, 30
animating spirit in women, 30
disturbed, easier to spot, 30
freed, 105
negative, 53
anxiety, 65, 72, 85, 136, 141, 157
archetypal
experiences, 93
powers,
encounter with, 49–50
going astray, 173–4
new approach to, 164
psyche and, 166
situations, young mother lover, 112